Pattern Recognition

Pattern Recognition

Mike James

BSP PROFESSIONAL BOOKS
OXFORD LONDON EDINBURGH
BOSTON PALO ALTO MELBOURNE

Copyright © Mike James, 1987

All rights reserved. No part of this
publication may be reproduced, stored
in a retrieval system, or transmitted,
in any form, or by any means,
electronic, mechanical, photocopying,
recording or otherwise without
the prior permission of the
copyright owner.

First published 1987

British Library
Cataloguing in Publication Data

James, Mike
    Pattern recognition.
    1. Pattern perception
    I. Title
    006.4 0327

ISBN 0-632-01885-2

BSP Professional Books
Editorial offices:
Osney Mead, Oxford OX2 0EL
    (*Orders*: Tel. 0865 240201)
8 John Street, London WC1N 2ES
23 Ainslie Place, Edinburgh EH3 6AJ
52 Beacon Street, Boston
    Massachusetts 02108, USA
667 Lytton Avenue, Palo Alto
    California 94301, USA
107 Barry Street, Carlton
    Victoria 3053, Australia

Set by V & M Graphics, Aylesbury, Bucks
Printed and bound in Great Britain by
Billing & Sons Limited, Worcester.

Contents

Preface	viii
A Note on the Programs	x
1 Pattern Recognition and Images	**1**
Image processing	2
Digitisation	5
Threshold selection	11
Predicate functions	14
Image processing hardware	15
2 Recognition and Classification	**19**
Recognition, classification and understanding	19
Classification and feature extraction	20
An introduction to classification	21
Models – the normal case	22
The division of the sample space	25
Linear classifiers	26
A summary	28
Classification as applied to pattern recognition	30
Other methods of classification	30
3 Grey Level Features – I Edges and Lines	**35**
Local features and detection	35
Similarity and correlation – template matching	36

vi Contents

    Detecting local features using templates – convolution   38
    Edge detection using templates   41
    Edge detection using gradient methods   44
    Model fitting   46
    Line detection   53
    Problems with local feature detectors   60
    The decision process – non-maxima suppression   61

4 The Frequency Approach   **63**
    Spatial frequency and the Fourier transform   63
    The Fourier transform   65
    Standard and optical transforms   75
    The convolution theorem   76
    Filtering   76
    Other transformations   81
    Fourier features   81
    Spatial v frequency methods – removing noise   82

5 Grey Level Features – II Segmentation   **84**
    Segmentation as pixel classification   84
    Segmentation by thresholding   85
    Regions from edges – line and curve detection   88
    Relaxation   90
    Texture   92

6 Binary Images   **102**
    Boolean operations on binary images   102
    Properties of binary images   103
    Binary edges: 4- and 8-connectivity   107
    Local Boolean operators   109
    Finding isolated points   112
    Shrink and expand – binary filtering   113
    Shape – area, perimeter and moments   116

Binary mask matching	117
Boundaries and shape	121
The medial axis and skeletonisation	122
Counting and separation multiple objects	129
Postscript	135
Further Reading	138
The British Pattern Recognition Society	140
Suggested Projects	141
Index	143

Preface

Our expectations of what computers can or should be able to do increase daily, and have already reached the point where it seems incredible that there are no walking, talking and seeing computers. In reality we can just about manage to produce the walking and talking computer, but the automation of vision is still a very difficult problem! This is not to say that no progress has been made, and character readers and similar devices are now reasonably common, but there is still a long way to go.

This book is an introduction to pattern recognition as applied to images and image processing and as used in pattern recognition, suitable for a one- or two-term course at undergraduate level. The topics covered are developed as logically as possible in a subject that is essentially a mixture of abstract theory and pragmatic solution, and wherever possible I have tried to emphasise the practical. As low cost image input devices are now available for personal computers such as the IBM PC, listings of BASIC subroutines have been included. The choice of BASIC rather than a more traditional language such as FORTRAN, or a more academic language such as Pascal, is partly due to the availablity of a low cost BASIC complier for the PC (Microsoft's Quick BASIC), and partly due to the simplicity of the language. If you prefer another language or another dialect of BASIC, the programs are very easy to convert. BASIC is like FORTRAN and the particular BASIC style used makes it look very like Pascal, or indeed like any block-structured lanaguage. Some suggestions for short practical projects based on the use and extension of the subroutines can be found at the end of the book.

Wherever possible I have tried to explain the methods in terms that are suitable for implementation on a parallel computer. These parallel algorithms do not always result in the most efficient programs when used with a standard serial computer, and as a result most of the subroutines listed could be replaced by faster versions based on serial methods. The reason for the emphasis on parallel processing is that it is the method that we would like to use if only the necessary hardware were cheaper! With the falling cost of hardware, it seems better to be prepared for parallel thought rather than confining ourselves to serial thinking.

The images used in this book were all prepared using an IBM PC and a commercially available frame grabber – the IMAGE 3C Frame Store, kindly lent us by Dave Hurst of Eltime Ltd, Unit D29, Maldon Industrial Estate, Fullbridge, Maldon, Essex (Tel: 0621 59500).

The programs were written in collaboration with Kay Ewbank and my grateful thanks are due to her. I would also like to thank Professor M. J. B. Duff of University College, London, and my ex-colleagues at the Image Processing Group, for my training in parallel image processing. Their CLIP series is still the most powerful range of parallel computers for image processing. Thanks are also due to my wife Sue for much of the research necessary to complete this manuscript, and to my editor Bernard Watson of BSP Professional Books for his patient encouragement throughout the project.

Mike James

A Note on the Programs

All of the programs listed in this book were written to be complied using Microsoft's Quick BASIC complier. All that is needed to use them is a few extra subroutines to perform image input and display. These are not included because they depend too much on the type of image acquisition system used. The subroutines could be converted to work with an interpreter such as BASICA or GWBASIC but this would severely limit the size of images that could be processed in a reasonable amount of time. An IBM format disk containing all the subroutines listed and others is available. Details can be obtained from Saturn Workshops, Askrigg, Leyburn, North Yorkshire DL8 3LB.

Chapter One
Pattern Recognition and Images

Giving a computer or a robot the ability to see, even in a very limited sense, is an important and exciting endeavour. In the past, the limitations of computer hardware, both in cost and size, restricted us to trying very simple techniques. Now computer hardware is rapidly becoming the least of our worries. Even a desk-top personal computer, with a few extras, can be used to try out most of the ideas of pattern recognition and image processing. Processing time for images of reasonable quality is usually a few minutes and this means that a specialised high speed computer is still required for a real time system. With the introduction of suitable LSI chips, even these special-purpose image processing computers are bound to become more accessible.

Pattern recognition is a general subject in the sense that patterns take many forms, from the shock waves recorded by a seismograph to the acoustic waves that constitute human speech. However, in this book, the main subject will be the recognition of visual patterns or images. This connection between pattern recognition and image has led to much overlap with *digital image processing* –the general manipulation of images using a computer. This book is mainly about pattern recognition applied to images, but many of the topics covered would not be out of place in a book on image processing. In many cases the methods of the two subjects are the same; it is just the purpose to which they are put which differs.

Images – pictorial patterns – are so common that it is not surprising that much of *pattern recognition* is concerned with them. To *recognise* an image is a term that means many different things to different people, so it would be unreasonable to expect a single coherent theory to emerge. If such a theory existed, then many of the problems in the wider field of artificial intelligence would also be solved, and pattern recognition devices would be common-place. This is not to say that pattern recognition has yielded no practical results; it is rather that a variety of approaches have been used.

There is a tendency for workers to invent their own approaches and theories in response to the particular practical problem with which they are confronted. On the other hand, in the absence of any confrontations with real problems, there is a great temptation to theorise using abstract mathematics. Such theories are usually all-embracing, but too general or difficult to be of much use. It is possible to pursue pattern recognition as a branch of abstract mathematics; it is also possible to pursue it as a theory-less branch of pragmatic engineering. The best approach is somewhere in-between. There is a great deal of theory that can be used to guide the exploration and eventual solution of a practical problem, but it is far from complete.

One of the difficulties of explaining the underlying theories is that pattern recognition often uses results from other subjects that are relatively easy to state but very hard to prove without relying on the main body of the subject's theory. Students of pattern recognition and image processing will benefit from knowledge of probability and statistics, engineering mathematics such as transforms and differential equations, computer science and diverse subjects such as psychology, photography, photogrammetry, computer graphics, electronics and space science. How much needs to be known from each of these areas depends on the exact application in hand, but the need to track down background information from other subjects is a constant requirement of most pattern recognition and image processing.

In this book the major ideas have been presented in such a way that their relevance, both theoretical and practical, to pattern recognition/image processing should be clear, but should more detail be required then additional reading will be called for. For example, in Chapter Four the theory and practice of the Fourier transform, filtering and the fast Fourier transform algorithm are described in sufficient detail for their workings to be understood, and to show how they apply to pattern recognition/image processing – but this is just a special application of the wider subject of digital signal processing. If you need more information or background reading then one of the suggestions in the Further Reading section at the end of this book should prove useful.

Image processing

The recognition of images obviously involves the use of a certain amount of special computer hardware to acquire and display images. The ability to process images using a computer is not only useful for pattern recognition; the general area of image processing covers computer graphics, image enhancement, image restoration, image analysis, image compression and even special video effects for television. The fact that there is much overlap in the hardware used for these different purposes has led to a certain amount of overlap in methods. Many of the techniques described in this book are found in other branches of image processing, doing slightly different jobs. This can be the cause of much confusion, so it is important to understand exactly why a particular technique is likely to help with the task of image recognition, as opposed to, say, image enhancement. On the other hand, some of the methods and applications of other areas of image processing are useful in the early stages of image recognition. For example, image enhancement and image restoration are attempts to improve the quality of an image that has been degraded in some way, and improving the image quality might make it easier to recognise.

Colour images

A two-dimensional image is an arrangement of colours within a finite border. We can simplify things a little by considering only monochrome images, as a full-colour image can be regarded as a mixture of three monochrome images – one showing the red content, one showing the green content and one showing the blue content. This three-colour representation of a full colour image is possible because of the way that human colour perception works. Given any colour it is possible to find a mixture of red, green and blue light that reproduces it. In this sense, colour vision is a three-dimensional process and any colour can be defined as a triple of numbers (r,g,b) that give the amount of red, green and blue light that have to be mixed to produce that colour. The way that these three colours mix can be seen in Fig. 1.1 which is usually referred to as a *colour cube*. The use of red, green and blue is not essential and any three independent colours (i.e. no one of them can be produced from the remaining two) can be used. For the purposes of pattern recognition, and image processing in general, the combination of red, green and blue is a good choice because these are the colours used in a standard colour video display. Thus a colour camera can be made to supply three signals corresponding to the red, green and blue components of the image, and a colour display will reconstruct a full colour screen when supplied with these signals.

Although it can be proved that three monochrome images can contain the same amount of information as a colour image, it is a matter of observation that a single monochrome image can contain all of the important information in a colour image. For example, it seems obvious that a well-known person's face will be as recognisable in a black and white photograph as in a colour photograph. This may be obvious but it is not something that can be proved. However, in nearly all practical cases a monochrome image will suffice and, as most computers are hard pushed to process such an image in a reasonable amount of time, most of pattern recognition theory ignores colour. The fact that a colour image could be processed as three separate monochrome images is often quoted as a justification for this approach, but there is no guarantee that colour processing will not require something extra. The point is that a

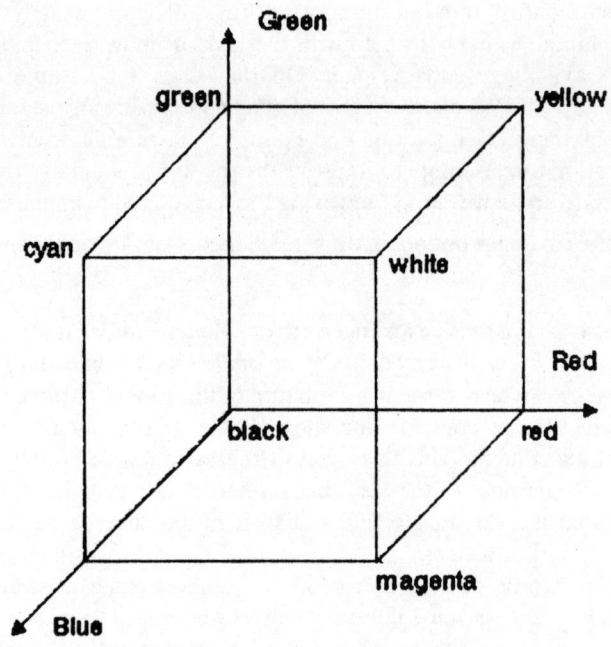

Fig. 1.1 A colour cube

colour image is not three independent monochrome images, but three highly related images and processing them separately may lose important information. The real justification for concentrating on monochrome processing is simply the observation that most of the information in an image can be represented adequately using monochrome.

Grey level images

Another name for a black and white monochrome image is a grey level image because each point in the image is assigned a single number that indicates how *bright* or *grey* it is. Mathematically a grey level image can be represented by a function of two variables $f(x,y)$ which gives a number a, $z=f(x,y)$, that corresponds to the grey level at the point x,y. As an image is usually only defined within a finite region, the function that represents it can be assumed to be non-zero only within a bounded region. By considering the physical characteristics of images you can be more specific about the type of functions that are needed to represent them. For example, as in any real image there will be a brightest and a darkest point the functions must be bounded – i.e. lie between some minimum and maximum value. In the same way, they can also be assumed to be non-negative, and integrable. There is much more that can be made of the relationship between images and functions and it is tempting to see the study of images as a branch of the theory of functions but, as will be explained later, just because something is represented by a mathematical object it is not necessary for all of the properties of that object to be relevant and vice versa. In particular, there are many operations that apply to functions when they are regarded as images, and even seem natural and obvious, but which are most unnatural as a part of the general function theory. For example, forming the histogram of brightness values is natural and obvious for an image but not in the general theory of functions. This does not mean that a knowledge of the theory of functions is not useful, in particular it is worth knowing about the elementary calculus of a function of two variables and about integral transforms such as the Fourier transform. These topics are introduced briefly as they apply to images in later chapters.

Digitisation

Another reason why the theory of functions is not entirely appropriate is that computer processing images are not represented as functions but as discrete arrays of numbers. In this respect practical images are more like matrices than functions. The process of converting an image into an array of numbers is referred to as digitisation. Although at first sight digitisation is a simple process it can be quite tricky. There are two components to consider – *spatial quantisation* and *grey level* or *luminance quantisation*.

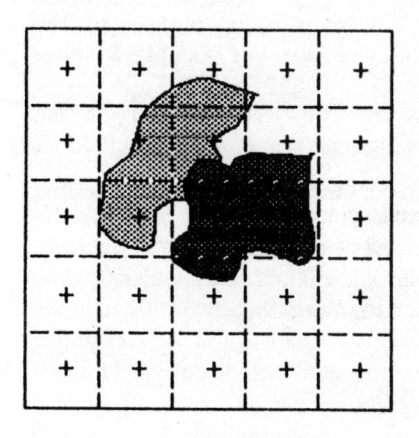

0	0	0	0	0
0	4	4	0	0
0	4	7	7	0
0	0	0	0	0
0	0	0	0	0

+ represents a sampling point

Fig. 1.2 Spatial quantisation of an image

6 Pattern Recognition

Spatial quantisation

Spatial quantisation corresponds to sampling the brightness of the image at a number of points, usually a rectangular grid. This spatial quantisation gives rise to an array of numbers A which can be taken to be an approximation to the original image f(x,y). Each element of the array a_{ij} is referred to as a *pixel* which stands for picture element. Figure 1.2 illustrates a simple sampling scheme.

This of course raises the question of how well A approximates f(x,y). If n^2 samples are taken at regular intervals within a bounding square then it is obvious that the approximation improves as n increases. Roughly speaking, as long as enough samples are taken, a spatially quantised image is as good as the original image. More precisely the original image can be reconstructed exactly from the digitised image as long as the sampling frequency (in samples per linear measure, e.g. samples per mm) is at least twice the highest frequency present in the image. This 'sample at twice the maximum frequency' rule is known as *Shannon's sampling theory* and the rate of sampling is called *Nyquist* frequency. (The ideas of spatial frequency are covered in Chapter Four.) Thus a digitised image obtained by sampling at the Nyquist rate contains as much information as the original.

In practice, Shannon's sampling theory is only a guide to the number of samples that have to be taken – in general signal processing applications over sampling by factors of 3 to 10 are not uncommon. The reason for this is that Shannon's sampling theory is concerned with the number of samples needed to recreate the original, not with the adequacy of the digitisation for any particular type of processing or presentation. In digital image processing, the number of samples is usually severely limited by the amount of storage available and the time taken to operate on the image. For example, a typical 512×512 image (image sizes are usually a power of 2) typically takes 128K of memory to store. (This resolution should be compared to that of a standard TV image of approximately 600×400. However, the perceived quality of a TV image is higher than these figures would suggest because the eye integrates information provided by 50 updated images per second.)

The number of samples taken is one aspect of spatial digitisation, but there is also the question of how the samples should be taken. Shannon's sampling theory assumes that the samples are *point samples* i.e. the value of f(x,y) at the sampling location, but other sampling schemes are possible. For example, you can average the value of f(x,y) over the small region (usually square) represented by the sample. Such sampling schemes can offer improvements in representation, but in practice the type of sampling used is generally determined by the type of digitising device available and this is usually some form of imperfect point sampling.

Grey level quantisation

Grey level quantisation is necessary because of the need to conserve storage and improve processing times. In principle, f(x,y) and the elements of A can take on any real value between 0 and MAX (the brightest point in the image), but in practice it is normal to restrict the brightness values to a finite set of integers. This conserves storage because only n bits are required to represent integers in the range 0 to 2^n. This means that, rather than the 16 or 32 bits needed to store a single real value, an image with integer grey levels in the range 0 to 7 needs only 3 bits per point. If 8 grey levels seem too few to represent an image, then 256 levels only need 8 bits per point, and this is still an improvement over storing a real 32 or 64 bit value for each point. A second advantage of a restricted integer range is that integer arithmetic and integer operations in general are simpler, and hence faster, than the equivalent fixed or floating point operations. Indeed, as storage requirements and processing times for each point are multiplied by the number of points in the image (for a standard serial computer at least), then it is only by the use of grey level quantisation that images can be processed in a reasonable amount of time.

We still have to describe how values of f(x,y) are assigned to an integer in the range 0 to N. The most obvious method is to divide the range 0 to MAX into N+1 equal intervals – *linear quantisation* - but it can be an advantage to use unequal intervals – *non-linear quantisation* – so that frequently occurring grey levels are covered by more integers. Using a variable or tapered quantisation can improve the average accuracy of quantisation.

There is also another reason for using non-linear quantisation which relates to the way humans perceive brightness. The eye has a logarithmic response to

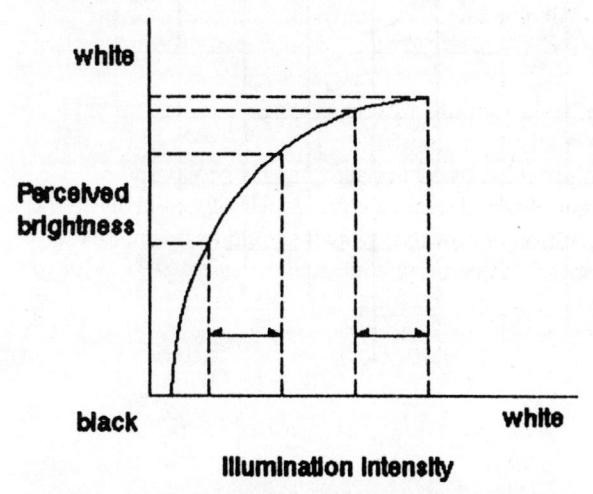

Fig. 1.3 The eye's logarithmic response to brightness

8 Pattern Recognition

brightness that makes it more sensitive to difference in darker tones (see Fig. 1.3.)

For example, if you look at a *grey scale*, that is, a set of bars of steadily increasing brightness, with even steps in brightness between each bar, then there will appear to be a bigger difference between the darker bars. If you look at a grey scale where the steps in brightness between each bar follow a logarithmic law, then the differences will be perceived as equal. Another way of looking at this result is to say that the eye is more sensitive to changes in dark regions than in light regions of an image, and this fact is sometimes made use of in image enhancement.

Because of this logarithmic response of the eye it is usual to quantise the brightness using a logarithmic scale. This allows more bits to be used to represent tones in the darker end of the range. Even so, if too few bits are used a defect called *contouring* can often be seen in dark slowly changing areas of an image. Contouring is the appearance of false edges in an image due to the inability of the grey levels to change smoothly from one value to another.

The majority of image processing equipment available today uses 8 bits to represent its grey scale. This provides 256 grey levels and, when combined

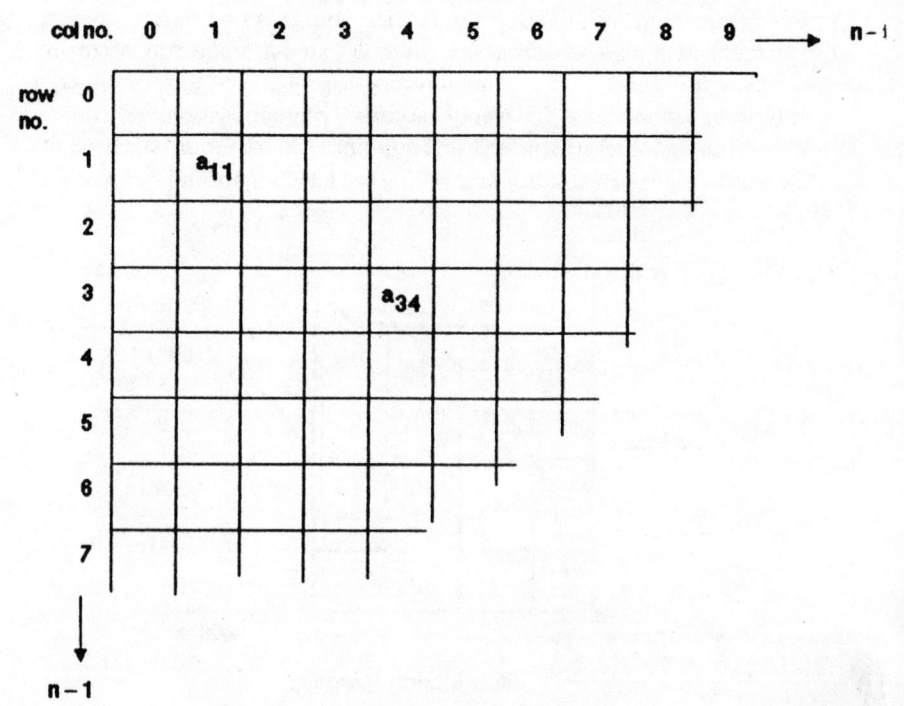

Fig. 1.4 Specifying points in an image array

with a logarithmic quantisation, doesn't lead to any visible false contouring. For some applications as few as 3 bits (8 levels) can give acceptable results.

Image storage and simple point processes

Following spatial and grey level quantisation, an image is represented by an array of integers, A. Any element of the array, or pixel, can be specified by giving i, its row number and j, its column number, that is, a_{ij}. It is usual to start the numbering scheme for both the rows and columns at 0 (see Fig. 1.4).

Once you have images stored in this form the most obvious types of processes to subject them to are based on simple arithmetic. For example, given two images A and B, their sum C=A+B is formed by adding together corresponding pixels, that is:

$$c_{ij} = a_{ij} + b_{ij}$$

Operations that combine together pairs of pixels from different images in this way are called *point processes*. This definition can be extended to include operations on the pixels of a single image A to give a new image C where:

$$c_{ij} = f(a_{ij})$$

and f is any function. For example, if:

$$f(a_{ij}) = ca_{ij} + b$$

where a and b are constants corresponds to a change in the *contrast* and average brightness of the image. Roughly speaking, contrast can be thought

Input device response curve

$f(a_{ij})$ needed to correct response curve

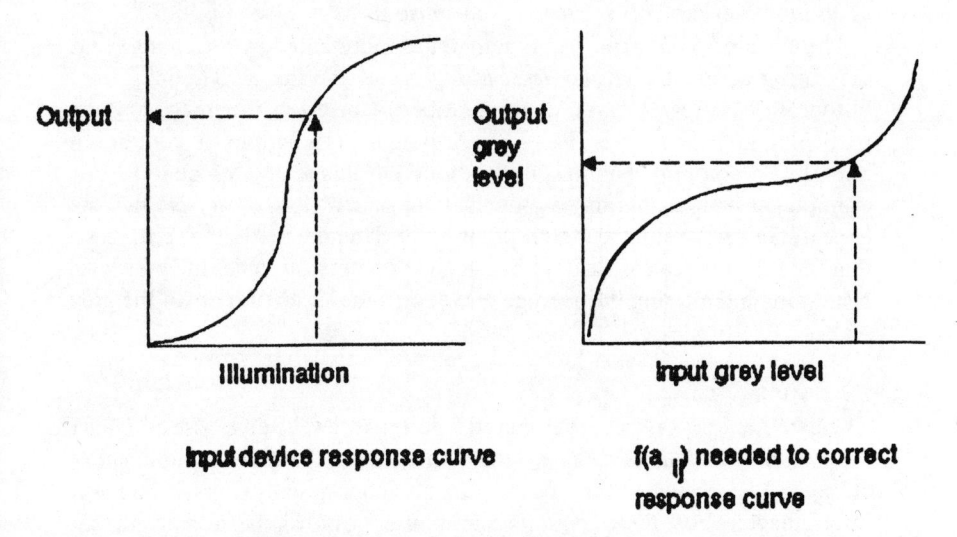

Fig. 1.5 Photometric correction

10 Pattern Recognition

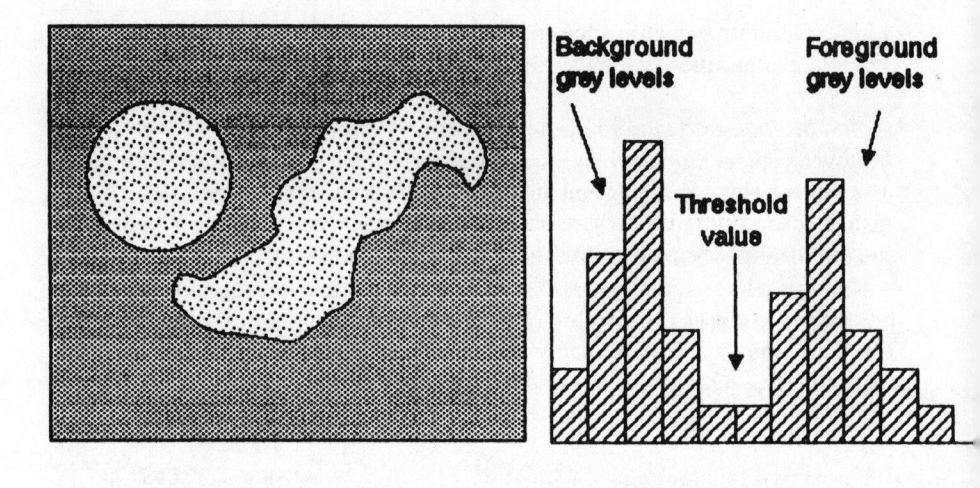

Fig. 1.6 Grey level histogram of image

of as the difference in grey level, and clearly multiplying each pixel by c will increase differences if c>1 and decrease differences if c<1. Adding b to each brightness value simply moves all the pixel values up (b>0) or down (b<0) the scale.

The function $f(a_{ij})$ can be defined by a table of values for each possible grey level. General functions of this sort can be used to correct or alter the response of an input device. This is called *photometric correction* (see Fig. 1.5).

The effect of point processes is sometimes represented by the change that they bring about to the *grey level histogram* of the image. The grey level histogram is simply a graph of the number of pixels in the image at each particular grey level (see Fig. 1.6). Although very simple, it contains a remarkable amount of information about the image and its quality. For example, if the histogram is bunched in one region of tones then its appearance can be enhanced by a point process that increases the contrast so that the full grey scale is used. Increasing the contrast stretches the grey level histogram and altering the average grey level slides it up and down the grey scale.

Binary images

The extreme case of grey level quantisation, two levels, gives rise to *binary images*. As you might imagine, binary images are the most economical of storage and processing time, and they are also conceptually simpler than grey level images. For these reasons more attention has been paid to the manipulation of binary images than to anything else. To convert a grey level image to a binary one all you have to do is select a *threshold value* and assign all grey values less than it to 0, and all grey values equal or greater than it to 1. Of course the result depends crucially on the value of the threshold. If the threshold is too high then all you see are a few bright peaks, and if the threshold is too low then all you see are a few darker regions. Neither setting provides a good representation of the original grey level image. What is surprising is that very often there is a threshold value which results in a binary image that is an adequate representation of the original. Of course, what is adequate depends on the purpose to which the binary image is to be put, and in this sense you can only begin to select a 'correct' threshold once you have specified the purpose of the binary image. For example, if you are trying to count objects then a threshold that shows the correct number of objects is good enough, but if you are also interested in their shape you may have to choose more carefully.

Threshold selection

Given a particular grey level image you may be able to select a suitable threshold by examining the results but for most pattern recognition tasks this method is not only inappropriate, but can also be misleading. In any complete pattern recognition system there is usually no scope for human intervention, and this means that even apparently trivial tasks such as selecting a threshold have to be automated. Many pilot pattern recognition systems give unusually good results because the researcher sets the threshold for each image, or perhaps just for difficult images and, when this is replaced by an automatic threshold selection algorithm, the performance is much reduced. Selecting the best threshold using all of the pattern recognition equipment inside any human's head is rather like handing the machine the difficult part of the solution and being pleased when it achieves the easy part. Any pattern recognition system that works with binary images should only be tested with images that have been created using an automatic threshold selection method – human optimised images are for demonstration or display only!

The most simple threshold selection algorithm is the *histogram method*. If an image is composed of reasonably evenly illuminated objects against an evenly toned background then a histogram of the brightness values will show two peaks – one for the foreground and one for the background. A histogram having two peaks is called *bimodal*.

If a threshold value is chosen to separate these two peaks (i.e. the bottom of the 'trough') then the background will be assigned 0 and all the foreground objects will be assigned 1, thus giving a good binary representation of the original. Of course, in practice it is very difficult to ensure an even

12 *Pattern Recognition*

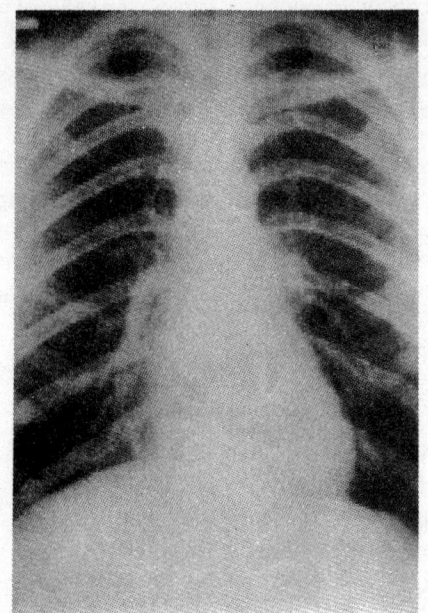

(a) A low contrast input image

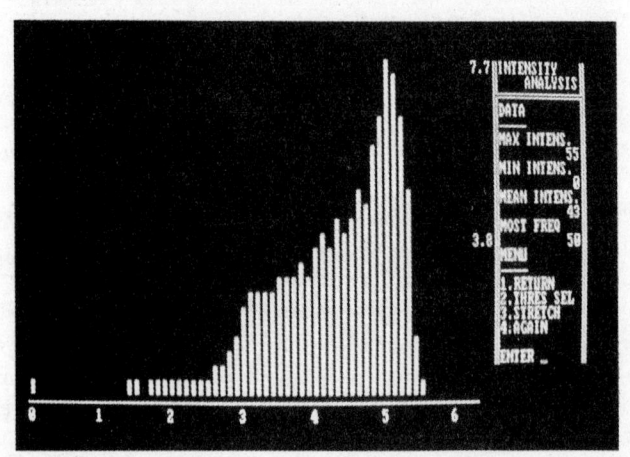

(b) Grey level histogram of (a) showing brightness value crowded towards one end of the range

Plate 1 An example of modifying image contrast by multiplication. On a video display the contrast enhanced image clearly showed details that were difficult to see in the original; however, this improvement in image quality is very difficult to render in a photograph

Pattern Recognition and Images 13

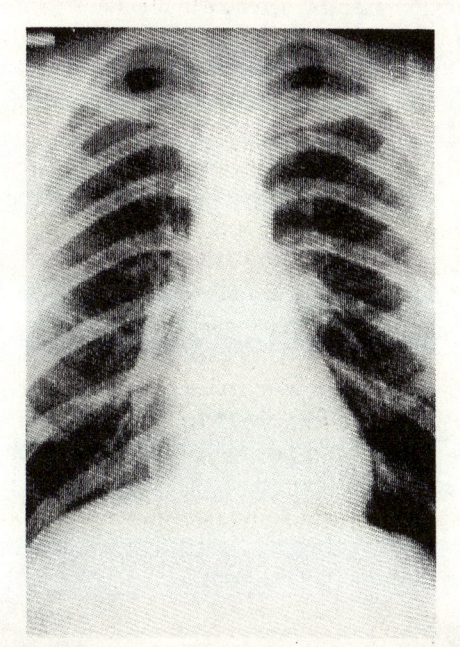

(c) A high contrast image produced from (a) by stretching the grey level histogram

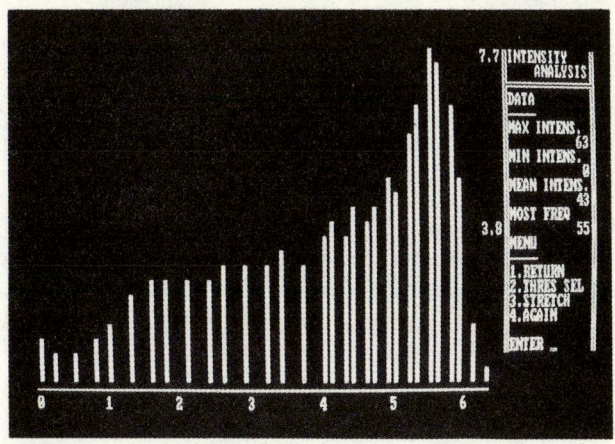

(d) Grey level histogram after stretching brightness values over the entire available range

14 Pattern Recognition

illumination of anything, and differences in orientation and colour result in a spread of grey levels among the foreground objects, which in turn make the bimodal form of the histogram less distinct. Most pattern recognition systems go to great lengths to obtain even illumination and high contrast. For example, the use of a fluorescent panel as the background can produce silhouette images that can be converted to binary by using a fixed threshold.

Other schemes for fixing the threshold generally depend on some special property of the class of images being processed. For example, some images have a guaranteed ratio of background to foreground, and for these a threshold can be selected which results in the same ratio of zeros to ones. However, it has to be admitted that for some images no single threshold exists that results in a binary image which adequately represents the original (see Fig. 1.7). For example, if you were trying to detect spheres then you might naively think that a sphere would produce a disc-like object in a binary image, but this would only be true if the original were very much brighter than its evenly illuminated background. In practice, a grey level image of a sphere may be shaded, in such a way that no single threshold produces a disc in the binary image.

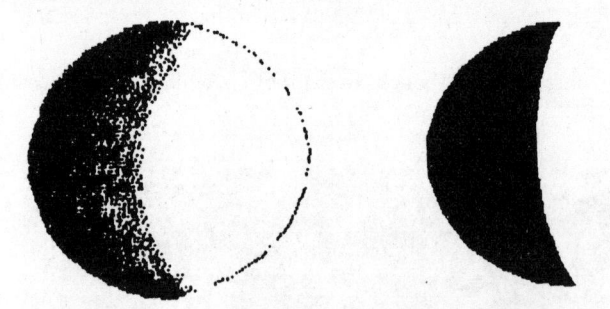

Fig. 1.7 The difficulty in selecting a threshold

To further complicate matters, when a human views a grey level image what is seen depends on what is recognised. In other words, a grey level image can appear to be an evenly shaded and quite clearly defined sphere making a good clear disk against the background, but in reality it is ill-defined. If often comes as something of a shock to view binary images taken at various thresholds of an apparently simple and clear grey level image – the results are usually worse than you would expect.

Predicate functions

In the previous section the problems of producing an adequate binary

(a) Original grey level image of a printed circuit board

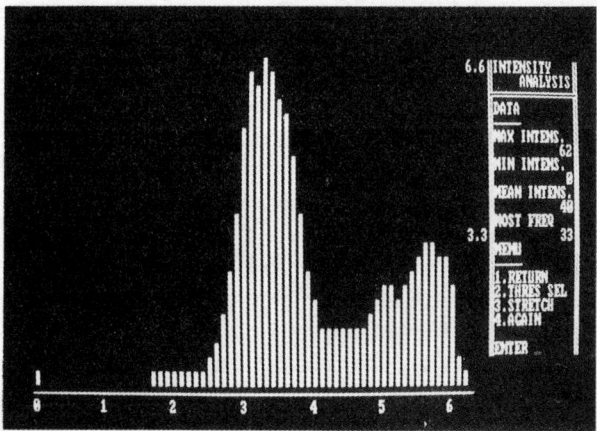

(b) Histogram of original image showing two peaks, one corresponding to the background and one to the foreground

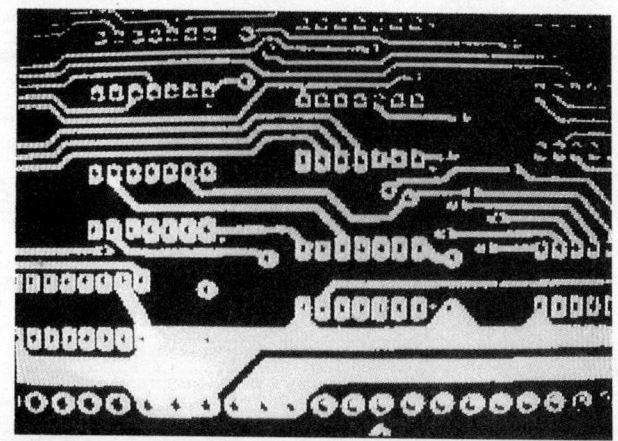

(c) Binary image produced by using a threshold determined by the histogram valley. Notice that some of the PCB tracks in the top right-hand corner have been lost even though they are clearly visible in the original

Plate 2 An example of histogram threshold selection

16   Pattern Recognition

image from a grey level original gave rise to the idea that a human might be able to assign zeros and ones to each point of the image to give a better representation. For example, if an image has a line running from top to bottom that becomes faint (but not necessarily invisible) then it might be impossible to select a single threshold that shows the line for its full length; nevertheless a human observer would see it so. Instead of thinking of creating a binary image by selecting a threshold you could envisage the more complicated process of deciding whether each point is background or foreground. Such a process is clearly not just dependent on the grey value of the point in question, and it may involve an examination of the entire image. So, to decide if a point is part of a line segment you will almost certainly have to enquire about the brightness values of surrounding points and even whether or not they are considered to be part of a line. A function that evaluates to either 0 or 1 is called a *predicate function*. This term comes from logic where a predicate function is one that assigns a truth value i.e. true or false, but any two-valued function can be considered in this way. In other words, a binary image is a predicate function that decides at each point of the picture whether it is a foreground or background point i.e. it *classifies* each pixel.

The construction of a predicate function that is an adequate representation of the original grey level image is in fact a large part of the entire pattern recognition problem. If you can construct such a predicate then you can, in at least a limited sense, recognise the objects in the image. In short, to decide whether a point is part of a line you might have to recognise the entire line. The subject of constructing such predicate functions to classify pixels will occupy much of the remainder of this book, but for the moment all that is necessary is that you are aware of the difficult nature of the task.

Image processing hardware

Image processing is a very demanding task for standard *serial* computers. A serial computer is one that can only carry out one operation at a time. As a result, a simple point process, such as the multiplication of each pixel by a constant, takes n^2 operations for an $n \times n$ image. Even if the multiplication is very fast, the time taken for the total operation on the image increases very rapidly. For example, a 512×512 image would require over 25 000 multiplications, which even at one millisecond per multiply gives a total time of 25 seconds! The only real solution to this problem is to use a *parallel* computer which is built in such a way that it can carry out more than one operation at a time. Ideally, an image processing computer would be composed of an array of sub-computers, one per pixel. In this way a process such as multiplying each point by a constant could be achieved in one step by each sub-computer working at the same time to multiply its pixel value by the constant. Using this sort of computer, the processing time depends very little on the size of the image.

Parallel computers of the sort described above do exist but currently they are very expensive. Useful pattern recognition and image processing can be carried out by conventional serial computers or indeed by personal computers. To provide image input or *image acquisition* for a personal computer all that is necessary in principle is a high speed A to D converter and a TV camera or some source of video input (see Fig. 1.8).

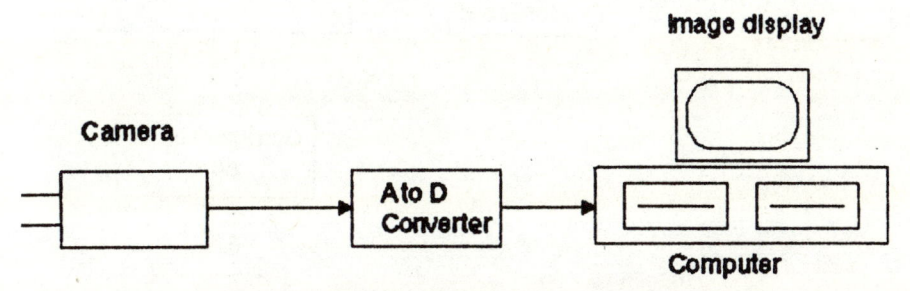

Fig. 1.8 A simple image acquisition system

In practice, this scheme has to be modified to take into account that most computers cannot read data into memory as fast as a standard video device can generate it. A TV frame is composed of a number of horizontal scan lines repeated every $\frac{1}{50}$th of a second – the *frame rate*. If the image being digitised is static, one solution is to digitise progressively lines from successive frames – i.e. first digitise line 1 from frame 1, then line 2 from frame 2, and so on. Of course, if the object moves then the resulting digital image will be scrambled in that each line will be a sample from a different image.

A more sensible arrangement is to use a *frame grabber*. This is a special piece of hardware that contains a high speed A to D converter, enough memory to store a complete digitised image, and a high speed communications interface to the computer (see Fig 1.9).

When signalled by the computer, the frame grabber digitises the next frame and stores the results in its internal image memory. The data stored in the image memory, that is the digital image, can then be read into the computer at leisure over the communications interface. As most computers are not able to display images of either the same spatial or luminance resolution it is best to incorporate a display unit. This takes the form of a high-speed D to A converter that can reconstruct a TV signal from the samples stored in the image memory. Thus a complete processing cycle would consist of grabbing the frame, transferring it to the computer, processing it and returning it to the

18 *Pattern Recognition*

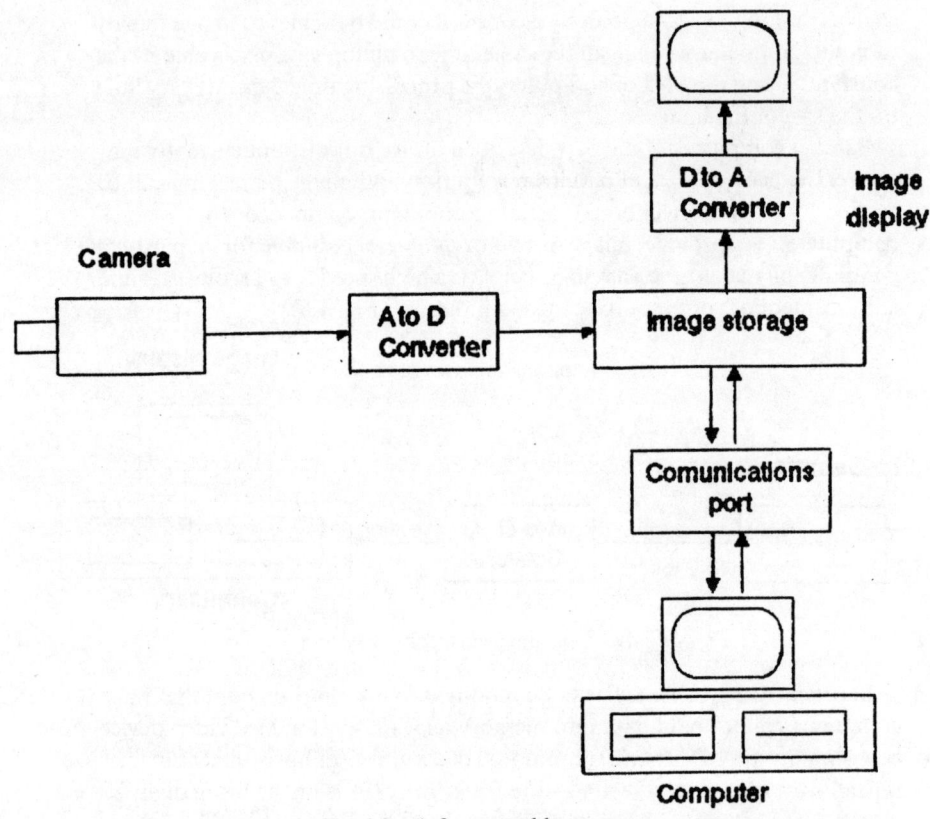

Fig. 1.9 A frame grabber system

image store for display. A frame grabber is one step towards a specialised image processing computer that can perform standard image processing tasks without the intervention of the host computer.

Chapter Two
Recognition and Classification

We are so good at recognising patterns of all sorts that it is difficult to see the nature of the problem in producing a program that will perform the same tasks. To us, things are clearly what they appear to be – a square is a square and a circle a circle – and it is difficult to fathom what makes them appear so clearly different without resorting to vague language such as 'a circle is round and a square is not'. In the context of pattern recognition, a description of how something is recognised is only useful if it is so complete and exact that it can be successfully programmed. Many of the early workers in pattern recognition (and psychology) relied on self-examination and introspection to suggest possible programmable methods. However, it seems likely that our knowledge of what happens during recognition is a long way removed from the more simple processing that makes the recognition possible. That is, our conscious processes are probably being supplied with information that is already the result of a great deal of processing! If this is true, then the only way to make any real progress with the problem is to try and find a general framework for recognition that does not depend on the particular problem in hand.

Recognition, classification and understanding

The simplest form of recognition can be found in applications such as character recognition, where an image is classified as a whole and as a particular letter. That is, the pattern recognition device is presented with an image, and successful recognition is merely the correct assignment to one of the letters A to Z, say. This is the *classification model* of recognition. It is the best understood and it forms the basis for more complex forms of recognition. A more subtle and complex form of recognition is *image understanding*. Given an image composed of a number of objects, there may be no obvious way of posing the recognition problem in terms of assigning it to a number of pre-defined classes. However, it may be possible to 'recognise' it in the sense of being able to name the objects that make it up and describe their relationships. The first part of this understanding i.e. naming the objects, is clearly strongly related to the simple problem of classification. If you can classify images into squares and circles this should be of help in detecting a square or a circle embedded in a larger image. The second part of this understanding, the deduction of the relationships between the objects, is more in the wider realm of artificial intelligence than that of pattern recognition. Thus, it can be seen that classification of images and the related detection of objects within larger images, as well as being useful objectives in their own right, are the first stages in the wider 'image understanding'.

Classification and feature extraction

The first stage in any pattern recognition task is usually referred to as *feature extraction*. Feature extraction is nothing more than a process of measurement, but this process can often be so complicated that it constitutes the main work of the pattern recogniser. The result of the feature extraction stage is a set of numbers x that are fed to the classification or decision stage of the recogniser (see Fig. 2.1).

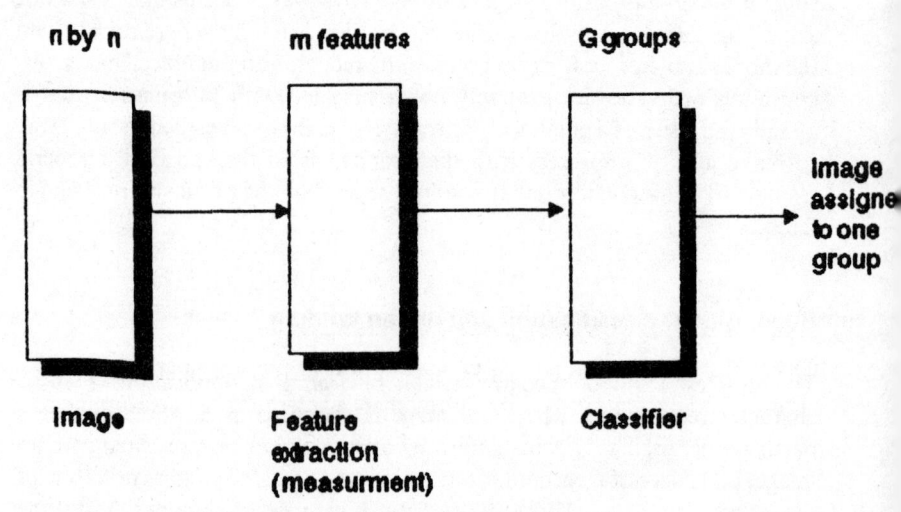

Fig. 2.1 A two-stage recogniser

Feature extraction and the selection of suitable features will be dealt with in detail later on. The classification stage is comparatively trivial, although it is properly based on some quite complicated statistics and probability theory.

An introduction to classification

Being able to classify an object into one of a number of groups is clearly something that might make a limited form of pattern recognition possible. For example, character recognition can be thought of as an attempt to classify a given image into one of the 26 letters of the alphabet. Classification theory has a long history in many different fields and it is important for anyone interested in pattern recognition. Being an essentially statistical theory it is first necessary to know a little about probability. Probability theory is dangerous in that it is very easy to make 'common sense' deductions about the probability of events and be very wrong! Fortunately the amount and nature of the probability theory that is necessary to understand the classification theory is not likely to cause such problems.

The *probability* of something, say, an event or happening, is usually written P(A) and read as 'the probability of A'. For example, P(heads) is the probability of getting heads on the toss of a coin i.e. .5 if the coin is fair. Very often we want to include the fact that we know something additional that affects the probability of the event. For example, the probability of throwing two heads in succession is .25 [P(two heads) = P(one head)P(one head)=.5 × .5=.25], but if we have already thrown one head then the probability of two heads is higher than this (it is in fact .5). This idea of the probability of one event given another event is called a *conditional probability* and is written P(A|B) and read 'the probability of A given B'. So, for example, the probability of getting two heads given that we have already thrown one head is P(two heads|one head on first throw) = .5

We can think of conditional probabilities as ways of summarising our knowledge of something after incorporating what we know about it. It is in this role that they occur in classification theory. If we know that an object must come from one of two groups, say, and on the basis of measurements $\mathbf{x}$ ($\mathbf{x}$ is a vector of measurements i.e. $\mathbf{x}=(x_1,x_2,x_3..x_n)$, we know that:

$$P(G_1|\mathbf{x})=.8 \text{ and } P(G_2|\mathbf{x})=.2$$

then it makes sense to conclude that the object is most likely to belong to group 1. As $P(G_1|\mathbf{x})$ is the probability that, given the set of measurements $\mathbf{x}$, the object belongs to group 1, we can think of it as simply the probability of group membership. This use of conditional probabilities to assign an object to the group that it comes from is the basis of all classification theory and it is known as *Bayes' Rule*. What is more surprising is that it is possible to show that Bayes' rule is the best that we can hope to achieve because it results in the smallest possible average error rate. Thus, in general, if we make measurements $\mathbf{x}$ on an object which may come from any one of m groups $G_1, G_2 ... G_m$ then Bayes' rule says:

22 Pattern Recognition

Assign to group i where:

$$P(G_i|x) > P(G_j|x) \text{ for all } j <> i$$

(that is, assign to the group with the largest conditional probability of membership).

Bayes' rule is such an obvious method of classification that it comes as something of a shock to discover that it is only the starting point of all our difficulties. The main problem lies in discovering the all-important conditional probabilities used by the rule to produce such optimum classification. In practice, they are nearly always unknown and have to be estimated from data gathered from each group. This gives rise to the use of estimated versions of Bayes' rule which may not perform as well as the ideal. It also gives rise to the possibility of several different estimates of Bayes' rule which have to be evaluated to discover which comes closest to the optimum. In pattern recognition there are many different *ad hoc* approaches to classification, each with their own particular appeal to commonsense principles. It is important to keep in mind when evaluating these procedures that, no matter how commonsense they are, it is their closeness to the optimum Bayes' rule that governs how well they perform.

Models – the normal case

One particularly easy way of estimating $P(G_i|x)$ is to assume that the probability of obtaining a given measurement within a group follows a known distribution. The probability of getting a given measurement from group G_i is $P(x|G_i)$ i.e. the probability of that measurement conditional on the object coming from group G_i, and there is a simple relationship between $P(x|G_i)$ and $P(G_i|x)$:

$$P(G_i x) = \frac{P(x|G_i)P(G_i)}{\sum_j P(x|G_j)P(G_j)}$$

This formula is known as *Bayes' law* and it provides the only really practical way of applying Bayes' rule. The probability $P(G_i)$ is known as the *prior probability* and is the probability of the object coming from group G_i without the benefit of knowledge provided by the measurement x. $P(x|G_i)$ is, in principle, something that can be determined experimentally. All you have to do is to construct a histogram of the relative frequency of occurrence of the different values of x for each group. For example, in the two group, single variable case, $P(x|G_1)$ and $P(x|G_2)$ might look something like this:

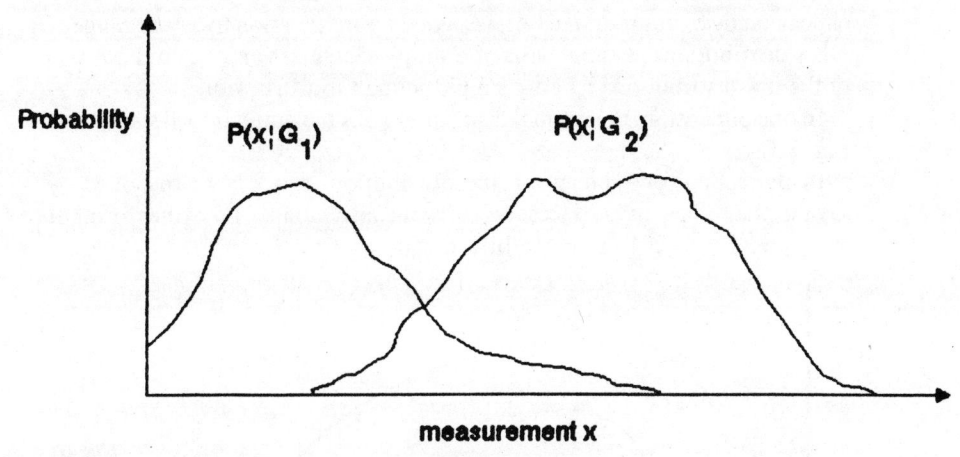

Fig. 2.2

If more than one measurement is involved, the number of samples needed to determine $P(x|G_i)$ increases rapidly and the only really practical solution is to assume that $P(x|G_i)$ has a particular shape as defined by a theoretical distribution.

The most common form of distribution to assume for $P(x|G_i)$ is the normal distribution with mean m and covariance matrix S. The normal distribution is favoured for a number of different reasons: it often does occur in practice

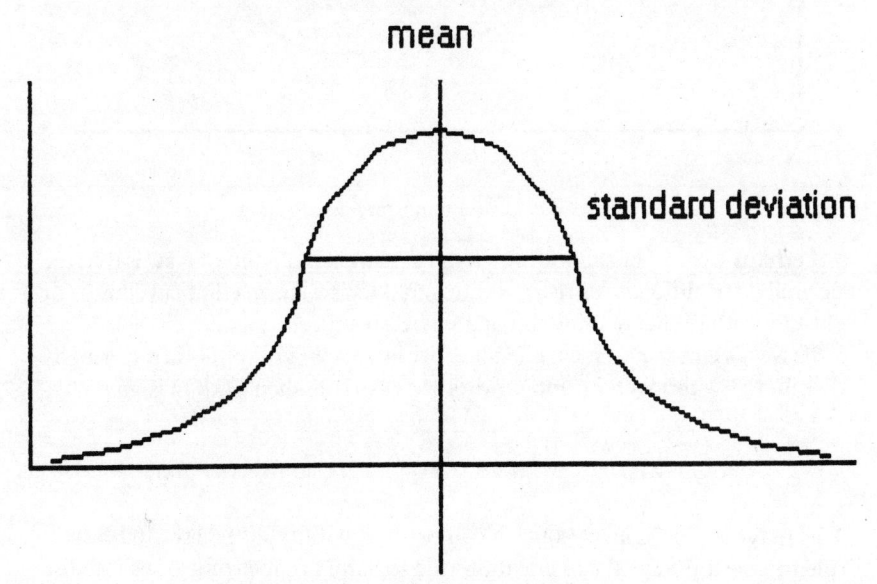

Fig. 2.3 The univariate normal distribution

24 Pattern Recognition

either exactly or approximately; it is a good approximation to a wide range of other distributions; it is the basis of a simple classification rule; and it is one of the few distributions that are simple enough to work with!

In one dimension, the normal distribution has the familiar 'bell shape' (see Fig. 2.3).

In more than one dimension the distribution can only be imagined by saying that lines or surfaces of constant probability take the form of ellipsoids. Figure 2.4 shows the bivariate normal.

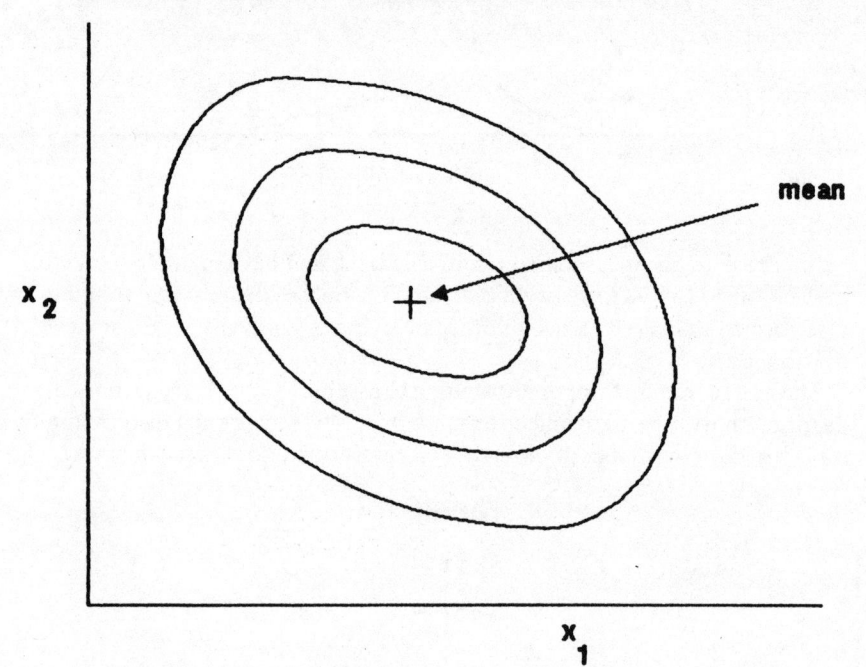

Fig. 2.4 The bivariate normal distribution

Perhaps what is most important from the empirical point of view is that the normal distribution gives rise to groups that tend to form elliptical clumps or clusters with points tending to congregate around the mean.

If we assume that measurements within each group G_i are normally distributed with mean m_i and covariance matrix S_i then $P(x|G_i)$ is given by:

$$P(x|G_i) = \frac{1}{(2\pi)^{n/2}|S|^{1/2}} \exp[-1/2(x-m_i)'S_i^{-1}(x-m_i)]$$

This may look complicated but it can be used within Bayes' law and Bayes' rule to give a practical classification rule for any number of groups (see the section on linear classifiers below).

The divison of the sample space

A particularly useful way to examine the nature of a classification rule is by drawing a diagram of the way in which objects with different ranges of measurements are assigned to the groups. For example, if we restrict consideration to two measurements and two possible groups, it is possible to draw a diagram that shows which regions correspond to objects that would be classified to each group (see Fig. 2.5).

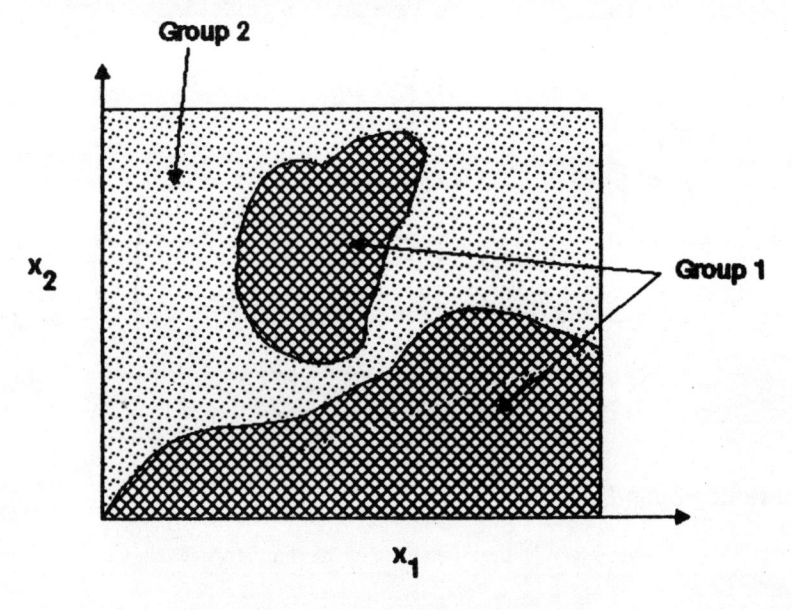

Fig. 2.5 Division of the sample space

In this diagram the region assigned to group 1 is simply all the points for which $P(G_1|x)$ is greater than $P(G_2|x)$. The boundary between the regions can be considered as a *decision line* (or surface). Points on one side are assigned to one group and points on the other side to the alternative group. This idea of a classification rule dividing up the sample space of possible values of x into regions belonging to each group can be extended to more than two groups and more than two measurements, with only an attendant increase in the difficulty of imagining the diagram. The important point is that any classification rule divides the sample space up into regions that belong to each group. It seems reasonable that classification rules that are simple to use result in simple divisions of the sample space.

Linear classifiers

The case of normally distributed groups each with mean m_i and covariance matrix S_i produces a particularly simple division of the sample space in that the decision surfaces are quadratic. This follows when you consider the shape of the groups that the surface divides (see Fig. 2.6).

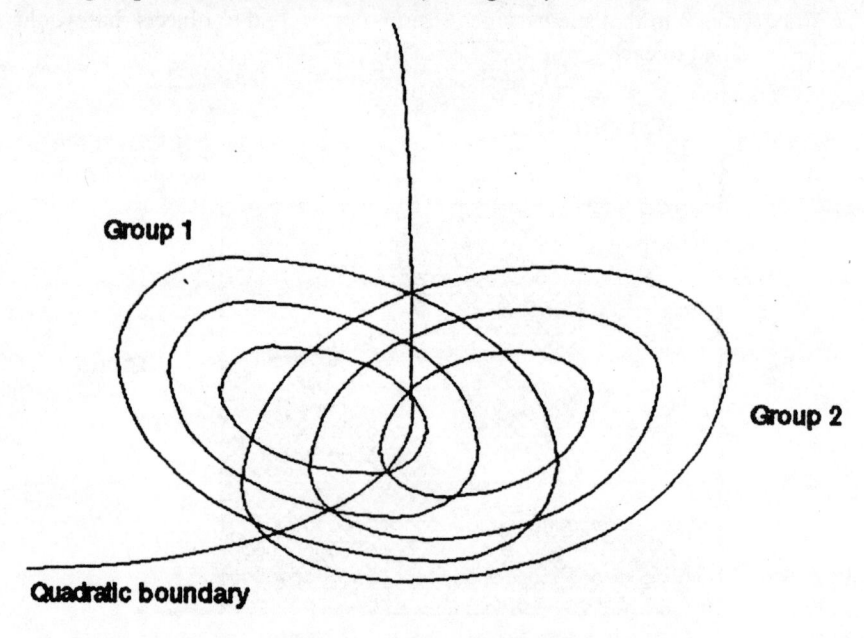

Fig. 2.6 Quadratic division of the sample space

A quadratic classification rule is fairly easy to use, but a great simplification results if we assume that the groups are not only normally distributed but have the same covariance matrices. This corresponds to assuming that each of the groups has the same overall shape. In this case, the dividing surface between the groups is linear. For example, with two groups and two measurements the dividing surface is, in fact, a straight line (see Fig. 2.7). Linear classification rules are particularly simple to use and it can be shown that in this case Bayes' rule is equivalent to evaluating an equation like:

$$f_i(x) = m'S^{-1}x - 1/2m'_iS^{-1}m_i$$

or, writing

$$c'_i = m'_iS^{-1}$$
$$c_0 = -1/2m'_is^{-1}m_i$$
$$f_i(x) = c'_ix + c_0$$

for each group and then assigning the object to the group that has the largest value of $f_i(x)$. The function $f_i(x)$ is usually referred to as a *linear discriminant function* and it is the basis of nearly all practical classification methods.

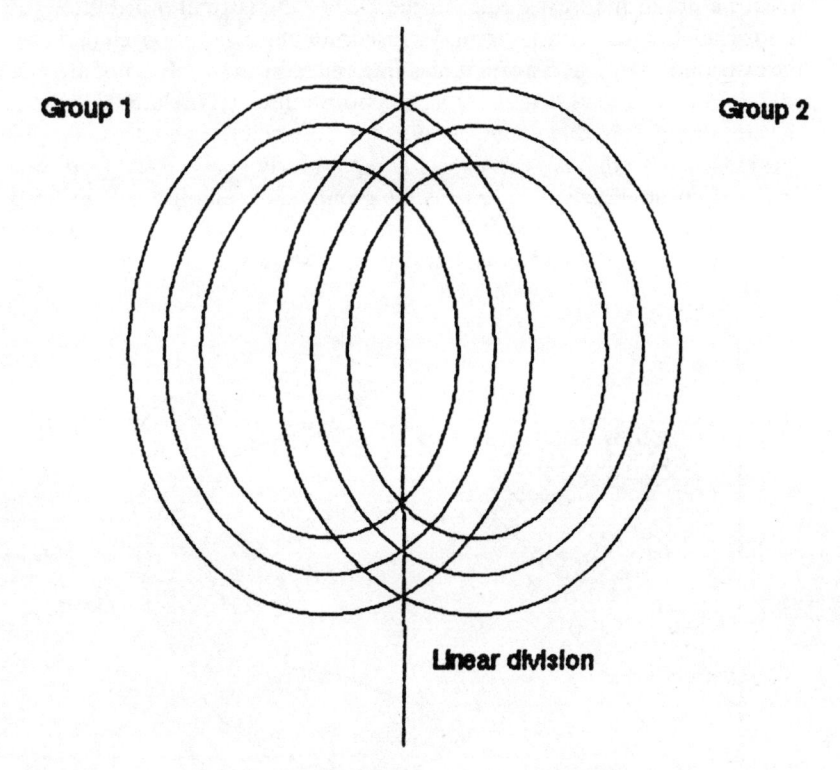

Fig. 2.7 Linear division of the sample space

What can be linearly classified?
Linear classifiers are by far the most common sort of classification rule used in pattern recognition (or any other subject for that matter). Usually linear classifiers are introduced by an appeal to the commonsense observation that two well separated groups can be classified using a linear rule (see Fig.2.8).

You could say that this is really an application of the principle that if two things are sufficiently different, then classifying or recognising them is very easy! In fact, it can be shown that as long as the groups have elliptical symmetry, a linear classifier is the best that can be achieved – that is, it is the Bayes' rule. Generally speaking, elliptical symmetry simply means that the groups are elliptical blobs in the sample space. More precisely a group has elliptical symmetry if its distribution is of the form:

28 Pattern Recognition

$$P(x|G)=K(A)f[\sqrt{(x-m_i)'A(x-m_i)}]$$

In this case, the normal distribution is of this form which accounts for the linear nature of the Bayes' rule. In the case of the normal distribution, the linear classifier takes the form of the discriminant functions given earlier. If the distributions are non-normal, the linear classification rule is not identical to the standard use of discriminant functions but closely related. However, the importance of this result should not be underestimated as, roughly speaking, it says that we can expect comparatively good results from well-designed linear classifiers as long as the groups show elliptical symmetry. If the groups do not show elliptical symmetry, it is certain that there is a better classification rule than a simple linear rule, as shown by Fig. 2.9.

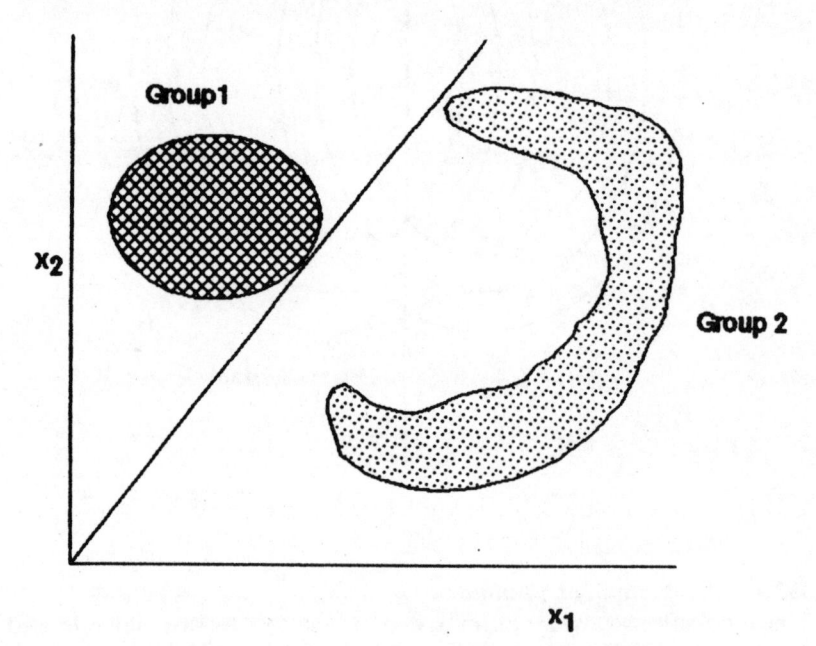

Fig. 2.8 Linear classification of well separated groups

In pattern recognition a major part of the problem is selecting measurements that are relatively easy to make and result in groups that show elliptical symmetry and hence are linearly classifiable.

A summary

The above discussion of classification is quite involved and relies on a large

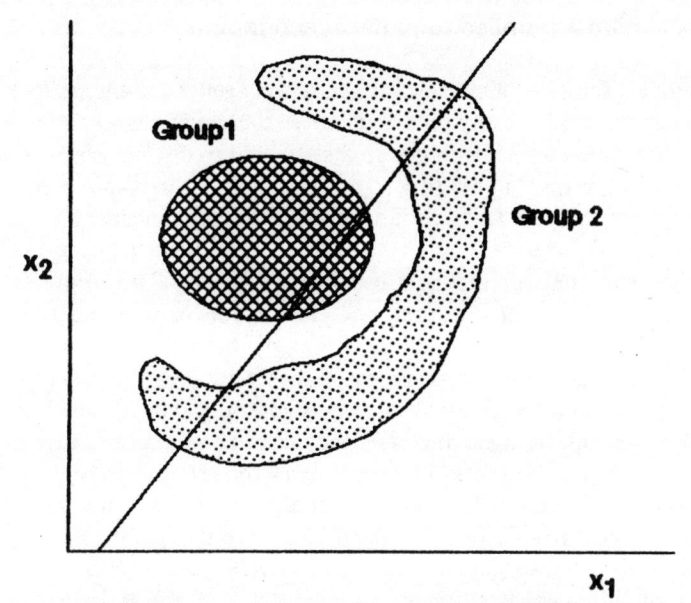

Fig. 2.9 Non-linearly classifiable groups

number of results from perhaps unfamiliar areas such as probability and statistics, so it is worth presenting a simple summary of the results so far:

(1) The best classification rule for average minimum error is Bayes' rule, but in general we do not know its exact form because the distribution of measurements in each group is unknown.

(2) If we assume that measurements from each group follow a normal distribution then the resulting Bayes' classification rule takes the form of a quadratic function.

(3) If, in addition to being normally distributed, each group has the same overall shape i.e. they have identical covariance matrices, then the resulting Bayes' rule takes the form of linear discriminant functions.

(4) If the groups are elliptically symmetrical then Bayes' rule is linear and related to, but not identical to, the linear discriminant functions.

(5) We can only expect a linear classifier to work well either with groups that are widely separated (when any reasonable rule will perform well) or when the groups are elliptically symmetrical or approximately so.

Classification as applied to pattern recognition

The above discussion of classification is entirely general in the sense that the measurements could be anything, and indeed there is no suggestion of how to obtain such measurements that would serve well to distinguish members of the different groups. In pattern recognition the situation is special in that we are at liberty to select from an almost limitless range of possible measurements that will be used in the classification rule. In fact, the problem of obtaining such measurements is usually as difficult, if not more so, than deriving a suitable classification rule. For example, what measurements would you make on images of the letters of the alphabet so as to make classification easy? If the chosen measurements are such that the groups are normally distributed with equal covariance matrices, then the ideal classifier, i.e. the Bayes' rule, is linear and takes the form of easily derived discriminant functions – but of course in nearly all cases the groups are unlikely to be normally distributed with equal covariance matrices. However, if the measurements can be chosen to make the groups well separated or elliptically symmetrical, a linear classifier can still provide good results. Even these simple conditions can be difficult to meet in practice. This is particularly true in pattern recognition, and yet linear classifiers are almost the only type in use! The reason for this is that linear classifiers are so simple to compute that any inefficiencies that their inappropriate use might entail are generally considered a reasonable price to pay. Having said this, it is worth pointing out that with care very good classification results can be obtained using such methods.

Other methods of classification

As already shown, the pure statistical approach results in a linear classifier under certain well-defined conditions. In pattern recognition we are often faced with the problem of having to construct a classification rule without having any idea of the distribution of the measurements in the different groups. In this case it is usual to search for a simple, i.e. linear, classifier which, while not promising to be the optimum Bayes' classifer, will be at least as good. Such approaches are usually referred to as *non-parametric* or *distribution-free* classifiers.

The best-known distribution free classifier is produced by the *linear training algorithm*, sometimes known as the *perceptron algorithm* (see Fig. 2.10). For simplicity only the two-group case will be considered. This assumes that the groups are sufficiently well separated for a sample from each group to be completely linearly separable. In other words there exists a dividing line (or

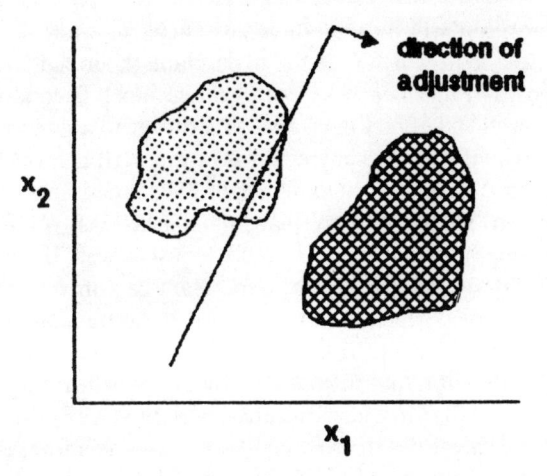

Fig. 2.10 Linear training algorithm

hyperplane) such that all the objects from one group are on one side and all the objects from the other group are on the other side. With just two variables finding a dividing line (if one exists) is quite easy, because it is possible to draw a two-dimensional scatter diagram and see the dividing line.

In more than three dimensions this manual process has to be replaced by an iterative search. The equation of the dividing hyperplane is given by:

$$\mathbf{w}'\mathbf{x} = 0$$

and if it separates the two groups $\mathbf{w}'\mathbf{x} > 0$ for all the objects in one group, and $\mathbf{w}'\mathbf{x} < 0$ for all the objects in the other group. Given a set of measurements from each group, we can check that these inequalities hold. If they do not, appropriate adjustments can be made to the elements of w and the check can be repeated. For example, if there is an object from group 1 on the wrong side of the hyperplane, then $\mathbf{w}'\mathbf{y} < 0$ (assuming that $\mathbf{w}'\mathbf{x} > 0$ for all objects from group 1) and the elements of w should be increased in an attempt to make $\mathbf{w}'\mathbf{y}$ larger. The most common way of doing this is to add a fraction of y to w. That is:

if y is from group 1 and $\mathbf{w}'\mathbf{y} < 0$ then update w by w + ay

and

if y is from group 2 and $\mathbf{w}'\mathbf{y} > 0$ then update w by w − ay

where a controls the rate at which the hyperplane is adjusted. The simplest version of this algorithm uses a fixed value for a. This procedure is repeated for each object in the samples until there is no change in w, at which point the hyperplane separates the two groups. Of course, there is no guarantee that

32 Pattern Recognition

this iterative algorithm will indeed converge. There may not be a linearly separating hyperplane in which case the hyperplane described by w simply oscillates in a position that nearly separates the groups! There are ways of optimising the search and of making it always converge to a reasonably good separating hyperplane, but more interesting is how it performs once derived.

If the two groups really are linearly separable, that is no object ever appears on the wrong side of the hyperplane, then the classification is perfect and any linearly separating hyperplane would do just as well. If, on the other hand, the groups do overlap, the derived hyperplane can only be optimum if it is the Bayes' classifier, which it can only be if the groups are elliptically symmetrical. The advantage of the linear training algorithm is that it can be used to give the impression that the pattern recogniser is 'learning' from the images that are presented to it. That is, it can be presented with examples from each of the possible categories which it classifies using the linear classifier. If it is correct, nothing happens. If it is incorrect, a human (usually referred to as the *teacher* or the *trainer*), can intervene and let the machine know of its error whereupon it modifies the weights using the algorithm given above.

Decision trees

There are some cases where, after some measurements, the classification of the object is so certain that probability and the Bayes' rule hardly seem necessary. For example, by counting the number of clearly-defined end points, the upper case letters of the alphabet can be classified into five groups, as shown in Table 2.1.

Table 2.1

\multicolumn{5}{c}{*Number of end points*}
0	1	2	3	4
B	P	ACG	E	H
D		LMN	F	I
O		QRS	J	K
		UVW	T	X
		Z	Y	

From this table it is clear that an upper case letter with one end point must be a letter P, therefore P(letter=P|end points=1)=1. That is, the probability of the letter being a P, given that you have measured one end point, is 1.

Recognition and Classification 33

Similarly, the conditional probabilities for the other groups, given the measurement of 0, 1, 3 or 4 end points, are also 1, and classification into one of these five groups is so certain as to be non-statistical. It is not that Bayes' rules does not work but rather that the classification is so clear that it is unnecessary.

Things are a little more complicated when a number of measurements are made. If each measurement splits the items up into different groups, by using them in combination a finer classification can often be reached. For example, if we include the number of T-junctions (i.e. the number of times two lines meet to form a T) in each of the upper case letters this can be used to make a finer classification (Table 2.2).

Table 2.2

\multicolumn{3}{c}{Number of T-junctions}
0	1	2
CDG	BEF	AHI
KLM	JPT	
NOQ	Y	
RSU		
VWX		
Z		

If you are told that a letter has two end points, the best you can do is conclude that it must be one of: ACGLMNQRSUVWZ (see Table 2.1 above), but if you also know that it has two T-junctions then it must be a letter A. (This is the only letter with two end points and two T-junctions!) This use of multiple measurements is more easily visualised as a decision tree. Each node in the tree corresponds to a measurement and there is a branch for each value of the measurement. Figure 2.11 shows the decision tree for the upper case letters classifier.

Decision trees occur in many pattern recognition applications and they can be much more complex than in this simple example. With a decision tree in mind, classification can be seen as a multi-step process. Each step uses a classification rule to divide the objects into increasingly smaller groups until classification is achieved. This approach also lends itself to an economical method of sequential classification by making only the measurements which are essential to classify the object in question.

34 Pattern Recognition

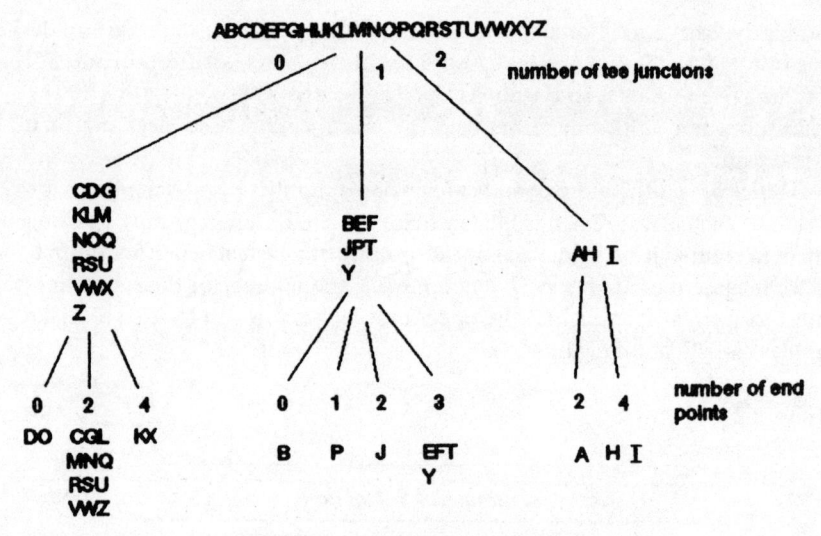

```
                    ABCDEFGHIJKLMNOPQRSTUVWXYZ
                   0         1      2    number of tee junctions

        CDG
        KLM              BEF
        NOQ              JPT            AH I
        RSU               Y
        VWX
         Z

       0  2  4         0  1  2  3      2  4       number of end
                                                  points
       DO CGL KX       B  P  J  EFT    A  H I
          MNQ                   Y
          RSU
          VWZ
```

Fig. 2.11 The upper case letter decision tree

Chapter Three
Grey Level Features – I Edges and Lines

The first stage in most pattern recognition tasks is feature extraction. Essentially a feature is a measurement that serves to distinguish or discriminate between a number of classes; however, the term also has a more familiar meaning, simply expressed as 'some perceived difference or attribute'. For example, the letter A is different from the letter O because it has a 'cross bar'. The horizontal line that, at least in part, contributes to the difference between the A and the O is almost something that is recognised in its own right – we can tell that it is present in the image and we can even say where it is. Another example should help clarify this idea. If we are searching for defects in a welded joint then the difference between an image of a bad weld and a good weld might be as slight as the presence or absence of a visible crack. The crack is a feature that serves to distinguish between two groups (good and bad welds), is clearly recognisable in its own right and has a particular location within the image. An identifiable feature that has a particular location within an image is usually referred to as a *local feature* and extracting a local feature is usually referred to as *local feature detection*. This chapter deals with standard methods of local feature detection, in particular with the detection of edges and lines.

Local features and detection

A local feature is a subset of pixels at a particular location within an image which form a recognisable object in their own right. For example, an edge, a line or any small geometric shape or arrangement of lines are all local features. Detecting a local feature within an image may be sufficient in itself to classify the entire image or it may have to be used in combination with other features as part of a classification rule. In some cases, simply detecting the presence of a local feature may not be enough because its position is also required. In some extreme cases the dectection and location of a local feature may be the prime objective. For example, if you are searching for military vehicles in

36　Pattern Recognition

reconnaissance photographs, then detecting a tank at a particular location is all that is required (even though this implicitly classifies the images into two groups corresponding to 'military vehicle not present' and 'military vehicle present').

In some ways, the concept of local feature detection almost seems just another way of stating the fundamental problem of image recognition. This is because what constitutes a local feature to one problem can be an entire image for another problem. For example, consider the problem of recognising individual words by detecting each one of the letters of the alphabet in turn. In this case, each letter is a local feature but in previous chapters we have considered the classification of images where each one is a single letter of the alphabet! In a sense, detecting a local feature is a more complex problem than straightforward pattern recognition, because you have the entire image to search through to locate the feature.

Similarity and correlation – template matching

Given a prototype of each of the groups into which you are trying to classify an image, a useful feature to use in a classification rule would be any measure of similarity between the object and each of the prototypes. This idea of using prototypes for each group is often referred to as *template matching*. Of course, the first problem is how to define the word 'similarity'. What exactly does it mean to say that two images are 'similar'? It is easy to see that two images are identical if their corresponding pixels are equal. That is A=B if $a_{ij}=b_{ij}$ for all i and j; however, two images that differ only in their contrast or overall brightness would normally be considered the same. That is, A is similar to B if $a_{ij}=k\, b_{ij} + c$ for all i and j where k and c are constants for the entire images. (Multiplying an image by a changes its contrast and adding c changes its average brightness.) A suitable measure of this sort of similarity has been used in statistics for many years – the *correlation coefficient*. For a pair of images A and B it is usual to work with the square of the correlation coefficient:

$$r^2 = \frac{[\sum_{ij}(a_{ij}-\bar{a})(b_{ij}-\bar{b})]^2}{\sum_{ij}(a_{ij}-\bar{a})^2 \sum_{ij}(b_{ij}-\bar{b})^2}$$

This quantity varies between 0 and 1 and is 1 when there is a perfect match between A and B in the sense described above. That is, when the correlation between two images is equal to 1, the two images are identical apart from brightness and contrast. As the value of the correlation coefficient begins to fall towards 0, the two images become increasingly different. Thus the value of the correlation coefficient can be used to classify an image by the simple process of computing the correlation between the image and a prototype from each group – the image is then assigned to the group with which it has the largest correlation.

Working out the correlation between the image and a number of templates can be very time-consuming if the formula given above is used. For example, if you are recognising letters of the alphabet and each letter is represented by a 10 × 10 grid of pixels, computing the correlation with just one prototype would take roughly 300 multiplications, 600 additions, two square roots and one division. However, much of this work can be avoided with a little preparation.

In practice it is usual to normalise the average brightness of all the images that are being processed making it possible to use the simpler equation:

$$r^2 = \frac{(\sum_{ij} a_{ij} b_{ij})^2}{\sum_{ij} a_{ij}^2 \sum_{ij} b_{ij}^2}$$

If each of the prototype images and the image to be classified are 'normalised' so that:

$$\sum_{ij} a_{ij}^2 = 1 \text{ and } \sum_{ij} b_{ij}^2 = 1$$

then the measure of similarity becomes:

$$r^2 = (\sum_{ij} a_{ij} b_{ij})^2$$

and this is simply the sum of all the products of corresponding elements i.e.:

$$= (a_{00}b_{00} + a_{11}b_{11} + a_{22}b_{22} \ldots a_{n-1n-1} b_{n-1n-1})^2$$

This is a much simpler quantity to calculate and, as long as the prototype and the image are normalised, it still varies between 0, indicating no similarity, and 1, indicating a perfect match. This sum of products form of the correlation is often used without normalising the images concerned. In this case, the un-normalised coefficient may be larger than 1 and its value is influenced by the size of both:

$$\sum_{ij} a_{ij}^2 \text{ and } \sum_{ij} b_{ij}^2$$

and so it is not simply dependent on the similarity of the two images.

Detecting local features using templates – convolution

Template matching as described above can provide a measure of similarity between two images, but as it stands it does not provide a method of local feature detection. For example, you can use template matching to classify an image into one of the 26 categories of upper case letters, but you cannot use it to detect all the occurrences of the letter A within the image of a page. The reason for this is that template matching is sensitive to a shift in position. If you take two identical images and calculate their similarity, the result will be 1 but if you shift one of them by a small amount, even though they are still in your opinion identical, their similarity will be less than 1. The solution to this problem is to compute the similarity of the image with a template shifted by every possible amount. If the image is identical to the template apart from a shift, then the similarity will be 1 for some position of the template.

This idea of working out the similarity of the image with a template shifted into every possible position is known as computing the *convolution* of the template with the image. The convolution can itself be considered to be an image the brightness of which indicates how well the template matches at that position. The equation for the convolution of an image A with an image B is given by:

$$c_{mn} = \sum_{ij} a_{ij} b_{i-m\,j-n}$$

This is, of course, an un-normalised measure of similarity, but it can easily be converted into a correlation coefficient. Thus, to detect a local feature, all you have to do is convolve the image with a template that is a prototype of the feature that you are looking for, and then pick out positions in the result which exceed a threshold value of similarity.

For a local feature, the template will usually be very much smaller than the image, and this gives rise to the notion of feature masks. For example, if you are looking for the letter A in an image that is 1 000 pixels × 1 000 pixels the template may only be non-zero in a small, say 5 × 5, area. Instead of thinking of convolving the 1 000 × 1 000 image with a 1 000 × 1 000 template containing a small letter A, you can consider working with a 5 × 5 mask. The result of convolution with the mask is still a 1 000 × 1 000 image, each element of which cmn is obtained by placing the top left-hand corner of the mask over a amn and working out the sum of the products of corresponding elements (see Fig. 3.1).

Masking is a natural and very common operation in pattern recognition and image processing. Although masking has been introduced as a method of local feature detection it has many other uses. In particular, it corresponds to the application of a filter to the image. This idea is explained in more detail in Chapter Four.

result at a_{00} = multiply and sum
= $m_{00}a_{00} + m_{01}a_{01} + m_{02}a_{02} + m_{10}a_{10}$
+ $m_{11}a_{11} + m_{12}a_{12} + m_{20}a_{20} + m_{21}a_{21} + m_{22}a_{22}$

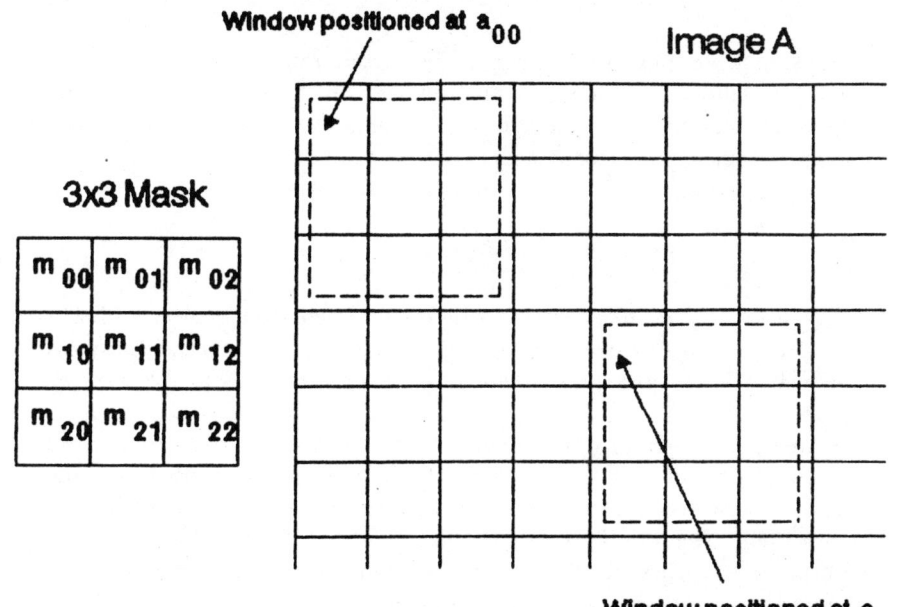

result at a_{43} = multiply and sum
= $m_{00}a_{43} + m_{01}a_{44} + m_{02}a_{45} + m_{10}a_{53}$
+ $m_{11}a_{54} + m_{12}a_{55} + m_{20}a_{63} + m_{21}a_{64} + m_{22}a_{65}$

Fig. 3.1 Convolution with a 3 × 3 mask

Ways of writing a convolution

The physical operation of convolving a mask with an image is performed exactly as described above but it is important to be aware of the different ways in which this can be written. Strictly speaking, the mathematical definition of the convolution of two images (or matrices) A and B is:

$$c_{mn} = \sum_{ij} a_{ij} b_{m-i\ n-j}$$

which corresponds to performing the masking operation described above after first performing a left/right and top/bottom reflection on the mask B. The reason that mathematicians define convolution in this way is to make certain results and theorems simpler (see Chapter Four). This usually doesn't make any practical difference because the masks used in image processing are usually symmetrical, but it can be a source of confusion if the masks are not. It is important to be aware of the fact that masks are sometimes reported ready to be used in a straightforward mask matching exercise and are sometimes reversed to comply with the strict mathematical definition of convolution.

A second way of writing the convolution arises from the fact that the mask is usually considerably smaller than the image, which makes it easier to write the convolution using a summation over the limited range of the mask's indices. That is, if A is a p × q mask:

$$c_{mn} = \sum_{\substack{i=0 \text{ to } p-1 \\ j=0 \text{ to } q-1}} a_{ij} b_{i+m\,j+n}$$

This is the equation which is used to implement convolution within a program. No matter how a convolution is written or implemented, what is important is that you understand the way it corresponds to the masking operation described in Fig. 3.1.

Another consideration when performing a convolution is where to store the result of multiplying and summing the mask and the image. In the definition given above the result is stored in the pixel in the top left-hand corner. However, this is not the only possible choice. Storing the result in the top left-hand corner introduces a diagonal shift to the whole image which can be undesirable in some applications. For example, if you are trying to detect edges, the high output indicating that an edge is present would be stored in the top left-hand corner of the area, even though you might consider the edge to be positioned in the centre of the mask. Clearly, in this case, it might be better to store the result in the pixel at the centre of the mask. Changing the pixel in which the result is stored causes no theoretical or practical problems.

A convolution subroutine

The following subroutine performs a general convolution of a mask, defined within the subroutine, with the image store in the array i% and places the result in j% both p by q. You might be surprised by the number of loops needed to implement a convolution. This is the reason it is a time-consuming operation.

```
Sub genconv(i%(2),j%(2),p%,q%) STATIC
   REM i% is input array j% is output
      both p% by q%
   REM setup m by n mask
   m=3:n=3
```

Grey Level Features – I **41**

```
      DATA -1,-1,-1,2,2,2,-1,-1,-1
      DIM m%(m,n )
      FOR k=0 TO m-1
        FOR l=0 TO n-1
          READ m%(k,l)
        NEXT l
      NEXT k
      REM do the convolution
      REM convolves mask dim m%(m,n)
      REM with image j%(p,q)
      FOR x=0 TO p%-1
        FOR y=0 TO q%-1
          j%(x,y)=0
          FOR k=0 TO m-1
            FOR l=0 TO n-1
              j%(x,y)=j%(x,y)+i%(x+k,y+l)*m%(k,l)
            NEXT l
          NEXT k
        NEXT y
      NEXT x
END SUB
```

Edge detection using templates

An edge is a clear example of a local feature, and edges are important in that their position is crucial to the location of boundaries between different regions of an image. An edge is a sudden change in the brightness of an image. This is a remarkably simple definition but in practice edge detection is quite difficult. Simple edge detection methods attempt to find edge elements, that is, places in the image where the intensity changes rapidly. Ideally an edge should take the form of a step, but in practice ramps and curves also occur. The typical shape of the edges in an image obviously depends on the type of object viewed, but it also depends on the type of imaging system in use. For example, if the image is digitised to a resolution that is in excess of the resolution of the image input device, there will be no sharp edges. Some imaging systems tend to blur edges that should be well within their resolution, others tend to 'ring', causing the brightness values at the edge to overshoot and oscillate. The best way to find out what the edge profile is likely to be in a given system is actually to measure its response to step edges of various sizes.

A mask to detect a step edge element is easy to construct. If the brightness on one side of the edge is a, and on the other b, the mask is simply:

42 Pattern Recognition

a	b

As the correlation between two images is independent of average brightness and contrast, this mask can equally well be replaced by:

-1	1

If you compute the correlation between this mask and any image you will find that it is always 1! The reason for this is that this definition of a step edge includes every possible value for a and b, including a=b, when most people would definitely conclude that there is no edge present! However, if the convolution of the mask:

-1	1

is performed without normalisation, the result at each point indicates the strength of the edge present. This is because convolution with this mask is identical to taking the difference between neighbouring pixels. That is:

$$c_{ij} = -a_{ij} + a_{i+1j} = a_{i+1j} - a_{ij}$$

Taking the difference between neighbouring pixels obviously leads to a result that indicates the size or strength of the step edge present at the location.

Simple differencing as described above will only detect step edges in one direction. To detect step edges in a variety of directions it is necessary to use more than one differencing mask. For example, the pair of masks:

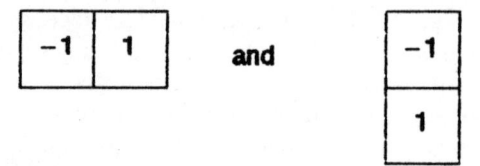

-1	1

 and

-1
1

will serve to detect vertical and horizontal edge elements.

Better edge detectors can be constructed if larger templates are constructed to take account of the fact that edge elements tend to occur together. For example, the output of the mask:

Grey Level Features – I **43**

−1	1
−1	1
−1	1

will give a larger result than the simple −1 1 mask if three step edge elements occur together to form a straight vertical edge. Larger masks are less prone to give large outputs where no edge exists but offer less discrimination between adjacent edges. If you calculate the correlation of this mask with the image you will find that, unlike the case of the simple −1 1 mask, it does give meaningful values. The reason for this is that to give a correlation of 1 with the larger mask, a 2 × 3 region of the image has to have brightness values given by:

a	b
a	b
a	b

where a and b are constants. Clearly, not all 2 × 3 areas of the image will be of this form. Even though the correlations are meaningful in this case, the result of simple (i.e. un-normalised) convolution is still used as an edge detector because this gives an indication of the size of the step edge detected.

A practical edge detection system based on the use of masks has to take account of the variety of the sizes of edge and of their differing orientations within an image. In general, this means using a number of masks of different size and orientation. Long thin masks give a finer angular resolution and hence more masks are needed to be sure of detecting edges at all angles. For example, the following are a set of five × five masks which have been used to detect edges at 0°, 30°, 60°, 90°, 120° and 150°:

```
-100  -100    0   100   100        -100    32   100   100   100
-100  -100    0   100   100        -100   -78    92   100   100
-100  -100    0   100   100        -100  -100     0   100   100
-100  -100    0   100   100        -100  -100   -92    78   100
-100  -100    0   100   100        -100  -100  -100   -32   100
             0°                                  30°
```

44 Pattern Recognition

```
 100  100  100  100  100        100  100  100  100  100
 -32   78  100  100  100        100  100  100  100  100
-100  -92    0   92  100          0    0    0    0    0
-100 -100 -100  -78   32       -100 -100 -100 -100 -100
-100 -100 -100 -100 -100       -100 -100 -100 -100 -100
              60°                            90°

-100  100  100  100  100        100  100  100   32  100
-100  100  100   78  -32        100  100   92  -78 -100
-100   92    0  -92 -100        100  100    0 -100 -100
  32  -78 -100 -100 -100        100   78  -92 -100 -100
-100 -100 -100 -100 -100        100  -32 -100 -100 -100
             120°                           150°
```

Edge detection using gradient methods

The failure of simple template matching to yield a useful edge detector leads to the use of masks which give results proportional to the size of the step edge present by simple differencing. This idea of using operations which give large results in regions where the brightness is changing rapidly can be generalised to produce a range of *gradient* methods. At any point in the image we can ask how fast the brightness is changing. However, the answer depends not only on the location but also upon the direction in which the rate of change is calculated. A suitable compromise is to find the maximum rate of change and its direction. For a continuous image f(x,y) this is easily found using vector calculus.

$$\nabla f = \frac{\delta f}{\delta x} i + \frac{\delta f}{\delta y} j$$

is a vector that points in the direction of the maximum rate of change and with a magnitude equal to that rate of change. In many ways all the different gradient methods result from attempts to find digital approximations to this classical result. For example, Robert's gradient is given by:

a_{ij}	b
c	d

$$\nabla a_{ij} = \sqrt{(d-a_{ij})^2 + (b-c)^2}$$

$$\text{angle} = \frac{-\pi}{4} + \tan^{-1}\left[\frac{b-c}{d-a_{ij}}\right]$$

Immunity to noise is improved if a larger area is used to calculate a gradient. For example, Prewitt's and Sobel's operators are defined on a 3 × 3 mask.

The eight neighbours of a_{ij}

a_0	a_1	a_2
a_7	a_{ij}	a_3
a_6	a_5	a_4

$$\text{Magnitude} = \sqrt{S_x^2 + S_y^2}$$

$$\text{Angle} = \tan^{-1}\left(\frac{S_x}{S_y}\right)$$

Prewit's gradient
$S_x = (a_2 + a_3 + a_4) - (a_0 + a_7 + a_6)$
$S_y = (a_6 + a_5 + a_4) - (a_0 + a_1 + a_2)$

Sobel's gradient
$S_x = (a_2 + 2a_3 + a_4) - (a_0 + 2a_7 + a_6)$
$S_y = (a_6 + 2a_5 + a_4) - (a_0 + 2a_1 + a_2)$

Gradient operators are used by applying them to an image and then taking a threshold. An edge is said to be present at a pixel if its result exceeds this threshold. One of the biggest problems in using gradient operators is in the selection of this threshold value. Notice also that these operators are not isotropic, that is, they give varying results from edges of the same strength with different orientations. There are many *ad hoc* variations on the gradient approach to edge detection and it is very difficult to establish their claims to superiority.

A subroutine for Robert's Gradient

Although Robert's gradient can be calculated using the general convolution subroutine given earlier, a faster subroutine can be created to implement it directly. This is true of most of the local operators described in this chapter. Subroutine roberts computes the Robert's gradient on the image stored in i%, placing the result in j% both p% × q%. Notice that only the magnitude is calculated and that in practice it is too time-consuming to compute its square root.

```
roberts(i%(2),j%(2),p%,q%) STATIC
     REM roberts cross gradient
     REM with image j%(p,q)
     FOR x=0 TO p%-1
       FOR y=0 TO q%-1
         d=i%(x+1,y+1)-i%(x,y)
         b=i%(x+1,y)-i%(x,y+1)
         j%(x,y)=d*d+b*b
       NEXT y
     NEXT x
END SUB
```

Model fitting

So far the local feature and edge detection methods described have a reasonable theoretical basis but they are all still subject to apparently *ad hoc* variations. For example, the correlation coefficient is a good measure of similarity between images but the most common edge detectors involve the use of un-normalised convolution of a mask with the image. One of the simplest approaches which explains many of these variations is based on model fitting. From the point of view of model fitting, both the correlation coefficient and the un-normalised convolution have a natural interpretation as a measure of 'goodness of fit' and 'strength of feature' respectively. A model of a local feature is simply a mask that defines the brightness levels of the feature using a set of parameters. For example, a 2 × 3 model of a step edge would be:

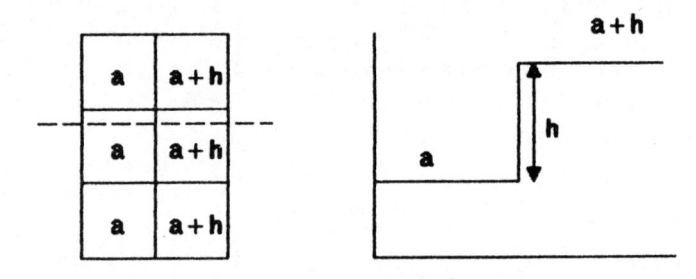

where h is the size or strength of the edge. Given this model of a step edge, we can ask if the brightness values of a portion of the image are consistent with it. To do this, the parameters of the model are adjusted to give the best possible fit to the actual values which occur in the image. The most usual measure of goodness of fit is *least squares*. That is, the parameters of the model are adjusted so as to minimise the sum of squared deviations. To be more precise, the least squares criterion demands that the parameters of the model should be adjusted so as to minimise:

$$SS = \sum_{ij} (a_{ij} - p_{ij})^2$$

where a_{ij} is the actual brightness level and p_{ij} is the brightness level predicted by the model. Statisticians will recognise this as a simple linear model for predicting y, a vector of measurements, as a linear combination of a vector b of parameters. If the predicted value of **y** is given by:

$$\hat{y} = Xb$$

then it can be shown that the value of the parameters, **b**, which minimise the sum of squared deviations i.e.:

$$\sum (y - \hat{y})^2$$

is given by:

$$b = X^g y$$

where X^g is the generalised inverse of X, and if X is of full rank then:

$$X^g = (X'X)^{-1}X'$$

The usual measure of how well the model fits is R^2, the multiple correlation coefficient. This varies between 0, a very bad fit, to 1, indicating a perfect fit. R^2 is given by:

$$R^2 = \frac{y'X'X^g y}{y'y}$$

The model of an edge given above can easily be written in the form y =Xb by simply writing the brightness values to be predicted as a vector y. For example, in the case of the 2 × 3 edge model we have:

$$\begin{bmatrix} a \\ a \\ a \\ a+h \\ a+h \\ a+h \end{bmatrix} = \begin{bmatrix} 1 & 0 \\ 1 & 0 \\ 1 & 0 \\ 1 & 1 \\ 1 & 1 \\ 1 & 1 \end{bmatrix} \begin{bmatrix} a \\ h \end{bmatrix}$$

$$\hat{y} \qquad X \qquad b$$

The best estimates of a and h can easily be found:

$$\hat{b} = (X'X)^{-1}X'\,y$$

$$= \tfrac{1}{3} \begin{bmatrix} 1 & -1 \\ -1 & 2 \end{bmatrix} \begin{bmatrix} 1 & 1 & 1 & 1 & 1 & 1 \\ 0 & 0 & 0 & 1 & 1 & 1 \end{bmatrix} y$$

$$= \tfrac{1}{3} \begin{bmatrix} 1 & 1 & 1 & 0 & 0 & 0 \\ -1 & -1 & -1 & 1 & 1 & 1 \end{bmatrix} y$$

which gives

$$a = \frac{(a_1 + a_2 + a_3)}{3}$$

$$h = \frac{(-a_1 - a_2 - a_3 + a_4 + a_5 + a_6)}{3}$$

as the best estimate of a and h.

48 Pattern Recognition

Ignoring the factor of $\frac{1}{3}$, these estimates can be implemented as the following convolution masks:

For a

1	0
1	0
1	0

and for h

−1	1
−1	1
−1	1

Both of these masks are fairly obvious in that the estimate of a is just the average of three pixels and the estimate of h is the average difference on each side of the supposed edge. The goodness of fit of the model is given by:

$$R^2 = y\,X'(X'X)^{-1}X'y$$

$$= y \begin{bmatrix} 1 & 0 \\ 1 & 0 \\ 1 & 0 \\ 1 & 1 \\ 1 & 1 \\ 1 & 1 \end{bmatrix} \frac{1}{3} \begin{bmatrix} 1 & 1 & 1 & 0 & 0 & 0 \\ -1 & -1 & -1 & 1 & 1 & 1 \end{bmatrix} y$$

$$= y\,\frac{1}{3} \begin{bmatrix} 1 & 1 & 1 & 0 & 0 & 0 \\ 1 & 1 & 1 & 0 & 0 & 0 \\ 1 & 1 & 1 & 0 & 0 & 0 \\ 0 & 0 & 0 & 1 & 1 & 1 \\ 0 & 0 & 0 & 1 & 1 & 1 \\ 0 & 0 & 0 & 1 & 1 & 1 \end{bmatrix} y$$

which when written out in full gives:

$$R^2 = \frac{1}{3}\,\frac{(a_1+a_2+a_3)^2 + (a_4+a_5+a_6)^2}{a_1^2 + a_2^2 + a_3^2 + a_4^2 + a_5^2 + a_6^2}$$

Notice that the goodness of fit cannot be calculated using simple convolution masks because it involves squaring pixel values. Using this model, the technique for detecting an edge would be to compute the goodness of fit at each position in the image. An edge corresponds to a goodness of fit close to one and at these positions the estimate of h, the size of the step edge, could be used to weed out 'weak' edges.

Grey Level Features – I 49

The two-stage procedure described above is rarely used in practice because of the need to calculate powers, an expensive process when repeated thousands of times. Instead, most edge detectors rely on just the estimate of h obtained using the convolution mask. This can lead to a great many false edges being detected which have to be removed by further processing, but this is usually considered a practical alternative. The modelling of local features is entirely general and can be used to detect any features, ramps, edges or lines with various profiles and blobs, which can be modelled in the manner described above. Other examples of modelling will be found later in this chapter.

The Hueckel operator – a sophisticated model

One of the best known and most sophisticated edge detectors based on modelling is Hueckel's operator. The edge models described in the previous section are all orientation specific. That is, to detect an edge at a particular angle you need to fit a model of an edge at that angle. In practice, a good range of edge orientations can be detected using a few models but this isn't entirely satisfactory. Hueckel's operator is an attempt to overcome this problem by the use of a general model of an edge that includes not only its step size but its orientation. To make this possible the edge has to be considered within a circular neighbourhood and the edge defined using four parameters – b the grey level on one side of the edge, h the size of the edge, and the radius r and the angle a of the edge in the circular neighbourhood (see Fig. 3.2).

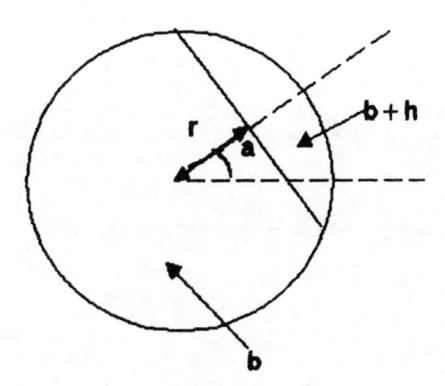

Fig. 3.2 The Hueckel edge model

In principle, using the Hueckel operator is easy – all you have to do is find the values of the parameters which make the model fit the section of the image that falls in the circular window. In practice, this is unfortunately very

(a) Original image

(b) Roberts gradient. Only the magnitude of the gradient is shown. Notice that it detects both horizontal and vertical edges

(c) Roberts gradient after local maxima suppression. This has thinned the detected edges but it has also introduced discontinuities

Plate 3 Examples of edge detection operators

(d) Result of simple convolution with −1,1. Notice the number of noise points detected as possible edge segments

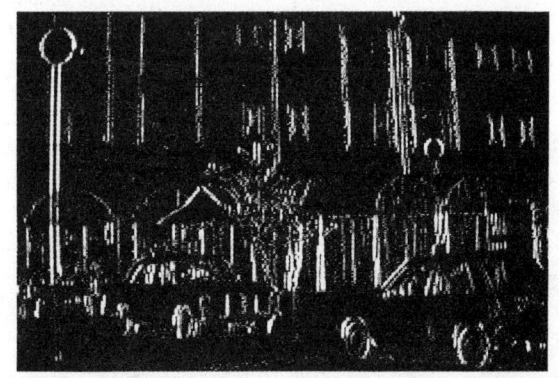

(e) Local maxima suppression applied to (d). This has removed much of the noise and thinned the detected edges. As the local maxima was taken over the same area as the mask the thinning is at right angles to the edge direction and so very few discontinuities have been introduced

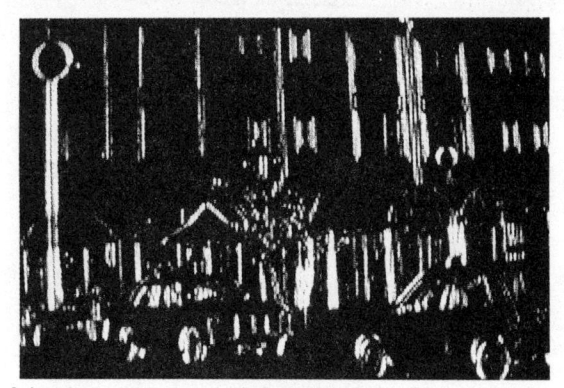

(f) Result of simple convolution with the mask −1,1
                                          −1,1
                                          −1,1
As this mask works over a larger area than that used in (d) it detects edges more strongly but it also responds to the same edge over a wider area. This results in the detected edges appearing thicker and fuzzier than in (d)

52 *Pattern Recognition*

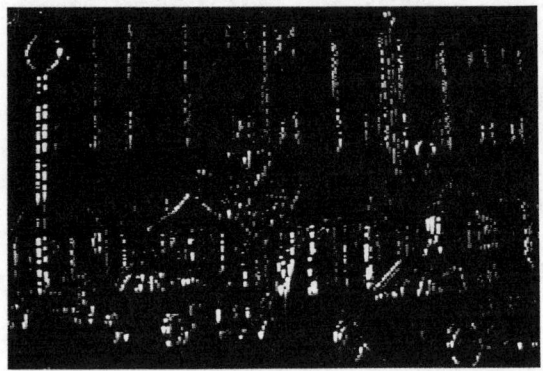

(g) Local maxima suppression applied to (f) thins the edges but now introduces some discontinuities because the mask extends in the direction of the edge as well as at right angles to it

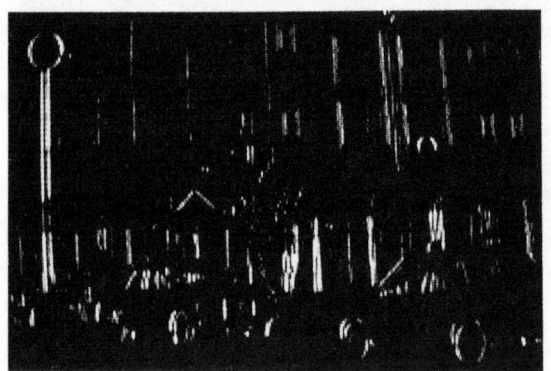

(h) The results of fitting the 3 × 3 linear model of an edge given in the text. This is equivalent to using the convolution mask used in (f) but in addition the points detected as edge segments in this image have to pass an additional goodness of fit test. The results show that fewer noise points are detected and the edges are thin enough without the need for local maxima suppression.

difficult, but Hueckel solved the problem by fitting a series expansion approximation (a radial Fourier series) of the model to the image rather than fitting the exact model. However, the resulting operator still yielded a measure of how well it fitted the actual image and estimates of all the parameters, including h, the step size of the edge. Hueckel's procedure was to declare an edge present at a point if the model fitted well and the step size was large. Hueckel's operator has long been thought of as the best that can be achieved as a raw edge detector but it is very time-consuming to compute and therefore not very practical. In general, most edge detection methods use simpler schemes for their initial detection phase and reject false edges by further processing.

Line detection

After edge detection, the most commonly encountered local feature detector is the *line detector*. Line detectors usually work by trying to find line segments which further processing can attempt to join together to form a complete line. In simple terms, a line segment is a small region of the image where the brightness levels increase suddenly and then decrease suddenly i.e. a line can be considered to be made up of a pair of edges in physical proximity. However, lines can exhibit a number of different types of brightness profile (see Fig. 3.3).

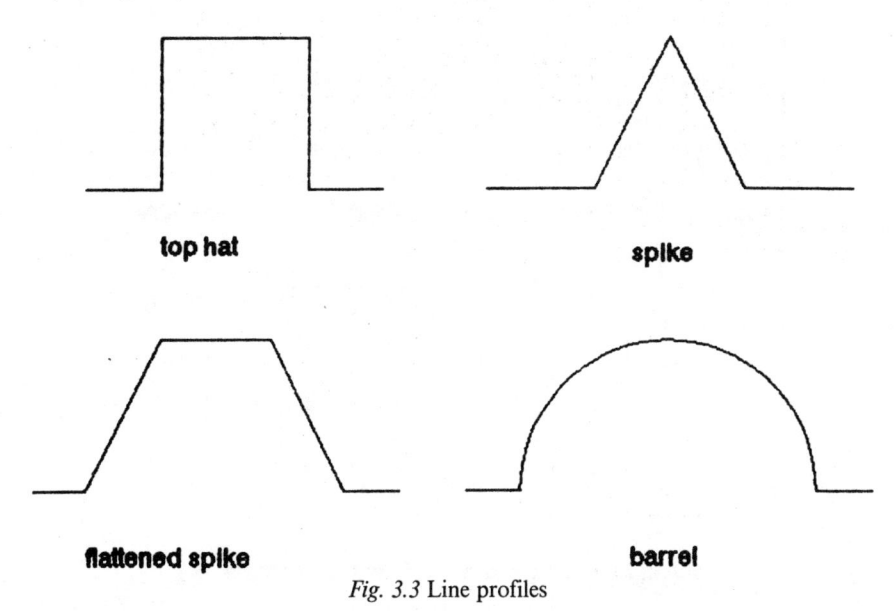

top hat

spike

flattened spike

barrel

Fig. 3.3 Line profiles

54 Pattern Recognition

Most line detectors are designed to respond most strongly to sharp lines with a top hat profile but, as is the case with sharp edges, these may not actually occur within the images being processed, due either to the nature of the images or to the image acquisition system. Once again, it is important to investigate the line profiles which actually occur.

The most obvious way to proceed is by constructing a model of an ideal line segment and then deriving estimates of its parameters and its goodness of fit.

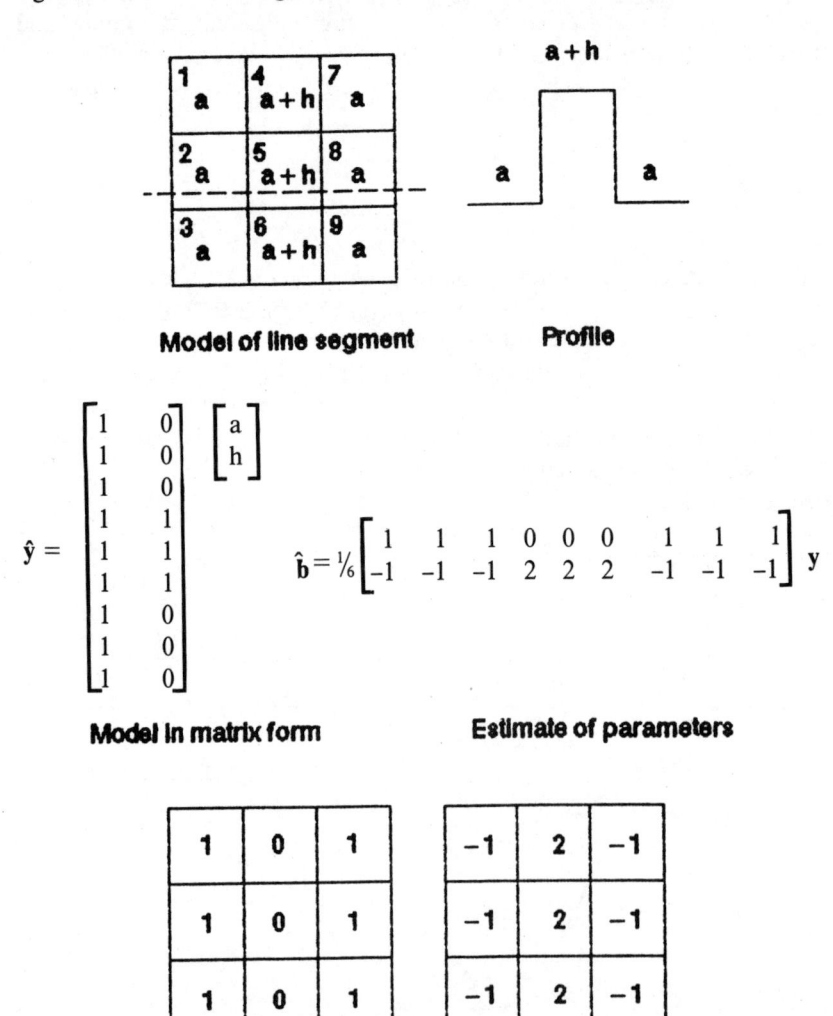

Model of line segment

1 a	4 a+h	7 a
2 a	5 a+h	8 a
3 a	6 a+h	9 a

Profile

$$\hat{y} = \begin{bmatrix} 1 & 0 \\ 1 & 0 \\ 1 & 0 \\ 1 & 1 \\ 1 & 1 \\ 1 & 1 \\ 1 & 0 \\ 1 & 0 \\ 1 & 0 \end{bmatrix} \begin{bmatrix} a \\ h \end{bmatrix}$$

$$\hat{b} = \frac{1}{6} \begin{bmatrix} 1 & 1 & 1 & 0 & 0 & 0 & 1 & 1 & 1 \\ -1 & -1 & -1 & 2 & 2 & 2 & -1 & -1 & -1 \end{bmatrix} y$$

Model in matrix form   **Estimate of parameters**

1	0	1
1	0	1
1	0	1

-1	2	-1
-1	2	-1
-1	2	-1

Mask to estimate 6 a   **Mask to estimate 6 h**

$$R^2 = \frac{1}{6} \frac{(a_1 + a_2 + a_3 + a_7 + a_8 + a_9)^2 + 2(a_4 + a_5 + a_6)^2}{a_1^2 + a_2^2 + a_3^2 + a_4^2 + a_5^2 + a_6^2 + a_7^2 + a_8^2 + a_9^2}$$

As in the case of edge detection, a line should only be supposed to exist at a point if the goodness of fit of the model is high and the estimate of h is large enough to make the line segment of importance.

In most cases this two-stage procedure is not used because of the time it takes to compute the goodness of fit. Instead the convolution mask to estimate h is used, large values signifying the presence of a line segment. The mask:

-1	2	-1
-1	2	-1
-1	2	-1

has been used for many years as a line segment detector for a variety of reasons. For example, it is often justified on the grounds that it is equivalent to taking the difference between nearest neighbours twice, and hence is a digital equivalent of finding the second derivative of the image. That is, forming the first difference between nearest neighbours gives:

$a_2 - a_1$	$a_3 - a_2$	$a_4 - a_3$	
$a_2 - a_1$	$a_3 - a_2$	$a_4 - a_3$	

and repeating the operation gives:

56 Pattern Recognition

$-a_1 + 2a_2 - a_3$	$-a_2 + 2a_3 - a_4$	$-a_3 + 2a_4 - a_5$
$-a_1 + 2a_2 - a_3$	$-a_2 + 2a_3 - a_4$	$-a_3 + 2a_4 - a_5$

Lines are areas of the image where the grey level gradient changes from a positive slope to a negative slope (see Fig. 3.4), and so computing the second derivative results in high values in these areas.

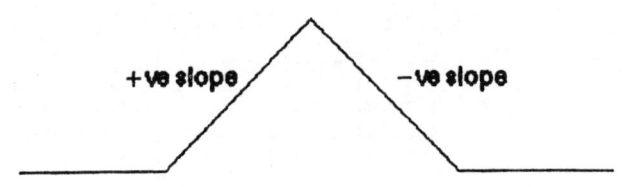

Fig. 3.4 A change of slope signifies a line

A subroutine to fit a line model

The following subroutine calculates the values of R^2 and the estimate of h given in the last section at every point in the p% by q% image i%. Thus the output is set to h if $R^2 > .9$ and to 0 otherwise. Thus only values of h corresponding to positions where the model fits well are returned in the p% by q% array j%.

```
SUB vline(i%(2),j%(2),p%,q%) STATIC
  FOR i%=0 TO p%-1
   FOR j%=0 TO q%-1
    REM calculate the estimate of h in fm%
    m1%=i%(i%,j%)+i%(i%,j%+1)+i%(i%,j%+2)
    m2%=i%(i%+1,j%)+i%(i%+1,j%+1)+i%(i%+1,j%+2)
    m3%=i%(i%+2,j%)+i%(i%+2,j%+1)+i%(i%+2,j%+2)
    fm%=m2%*2-m1%-m3%
    REM calculate R squared in r2
    tm%=i%(i%,j%)*i%(i%,j%)+i%(i%+1,j%)*i%(i%+1,j%)
        +i%(i%+2,j%)*i%(i%+2,j% )
    tm%=tm%+i%(i%,j%+1)*i%(i%,j%+1)
        +i%(i%+1,j%+1)*i%(i%+1,j%+1)
```

```
    tm%=tm%+i%(i%+2,j%+1)*i%(i%+2,j%+1)
         +i%(i%,j%+2)*i%(i%,j%+2)
    tm%=tm%+i%(i%+1,j%+2)*i%(i%+1,j%+2)
         +i%(i%+2,j%+2)*i%(i%+2,j%+2)
    REM check for division by zero
    IF tm%<>0 THEN r2=(((m1%+m3%)
                 *(m1%+m3%))+2*(m2%*m2%))/tm%/6
              ELSE r2=0
    REM reject values of h where r squared
        is less than 0.9
    IF r2<0.9 THEN j%(i%,j%)=0
              ELSE j%(i%,j%)=fm%
   NEXT j%
  NEXT i%
END SUB
```

Other second derivative operators – the Laplacian

The fact that computing the second derivative is useful in detecting lines suggests looking for digital approximations to the classical second derivative operators of traditional calculus. The mask $-1, 2, -1$ can be thought of as an approximation to the one-dimensional second derivative operator. The standard two-dimensional second derivative operator is the *Laplacian*:

$$\nabla^2 f = \frac{\delta^2 f}{\delta x^2} + \frac{\delta^2 f}{\delta y^2}$$

There are a range of possible choices in forming a digital approximation to the Laplacian. Two standard masks are:

0	-1	0
-1	4	-1
0	-1	0

-1	-1	-1
-1	8	-1
-1	-1	-1

Both of these masks give a large output in a region where the grey level gradient is changing rapidly. Another way of thinking about the Laplacian is to note that it is proportional to the difference between the grey level of the central pixel and the average in the region. In this sense the Laplacian gives an output that shows how unlike the local average a pixel is.

58 Pattern Recognition

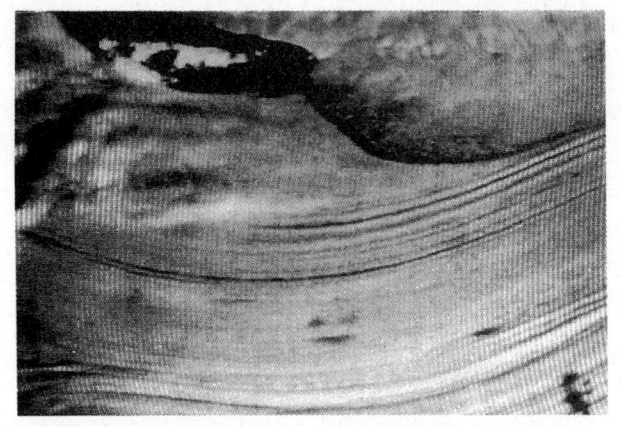

(a) Original satellite image of a glacier showing lines of flow

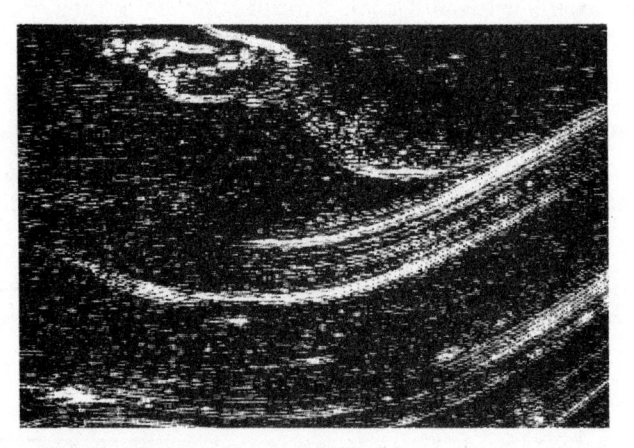

(b) Line detection by convolution with −1,2,−1
−1,2,−1
−1,2,−1

Notice the large number of noise points and the strong response from the edges of the rock in the top left-hand corner

Plate 4 Examples of line detection

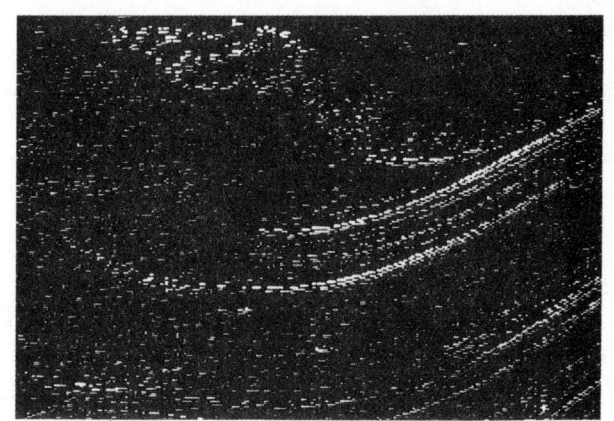

(c) Local maxima suppression applied to (b). As in the case of the edge detection examples this thins the lines and removes many noise points but introduces discontinuities. Also notice that the edges in the top left-hand corner are not removed

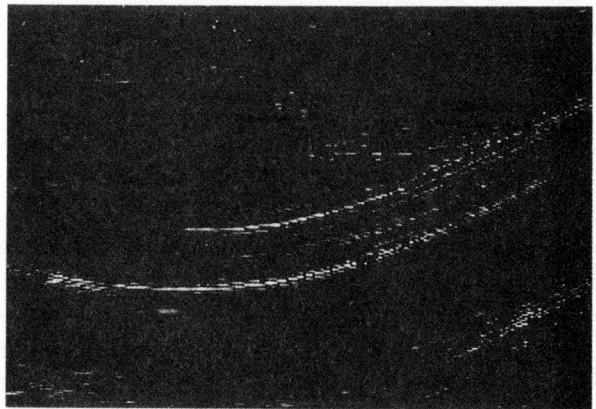

(d) Results of fitting the linear model of a horizontal 'top hat' line profile given in the text. This is equivalent to convolving the image with the mask used in (b) but with the addition of a goodness of fit criterion. Notice that this not only reduces the number of noise points and produces thin lines it also does not misidentify the edges in the top left-hand corner as lines

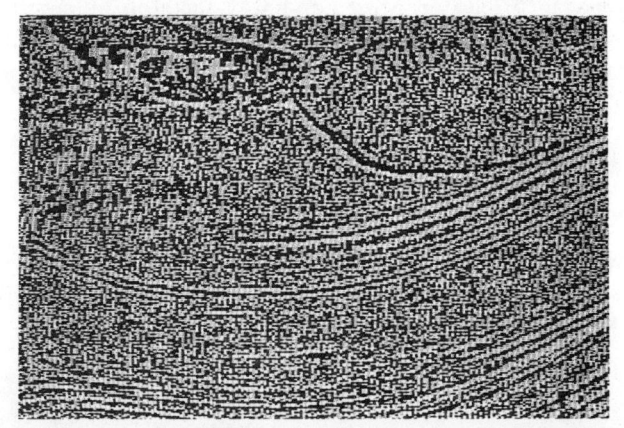

(e) Result of applying the Laplacian with positive and zero points shown as white and negative points shown as black. This simple representation gives an impression of the 'zero crossing' points as regions where black and white meet.

60 Pattern Recognition

Problems with local feature detectors

As already mentioned, in most cases local feature detection proceeds using only a convolution mask and this causes a number of problems. The convolution operation is linear and this means that a detector will respond to its target feature when it is present in combination with other features. For example, a line added to a step edge results in a brightness profile that is neither an edge nor a line (see Fig. 3.5) and, even though this doesn't look like the ideal 'top hat' line profile, the line detector still gives a high output.

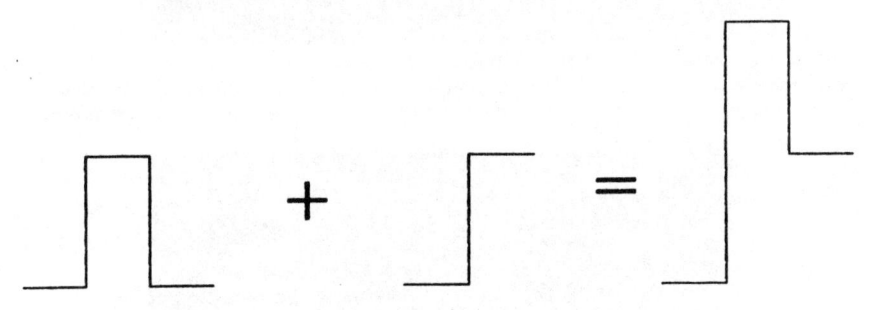

Fig. 3.5 A line added to an edge

The line detector also responds to other features in proportion to their contrast. For example, a step edge of height h produces a maximum output of h and a line of height h produces a maximum output of 2h. It is obvious that while the detector responds more strongly to a line than an edge, an edge of sufficiently high contrast can produce a larger output than a low contrast line. This problem is completely overcome by using the goodness of fit measure to screen out points that do not have the correct form to be a line segment, before examining the outputs of the convolution mask. Another solution is to move away from strictly linear operators. Non-linear operators are potentially more powerful but we do not have a well developed theory to account for their behaviour. Most non-linear operators attempt to add an easy measure of goodness of fit to the use of the standard convolution mask for the feature. For example, in the case of the line detector, the non-linear operator:

$$a_{ij} < a_{i+1j} \quad a_{ij} > a_{i+2j}$$
$$a_{ij+1} < a_{i+1j+1} \quad a_{ij+1} > a_{i+2j+1}$$
$$a_{ij+2} < a_{i+1j+2} \quad a_{ij+2} > a_{i+2j+2}$$

avoids giving high outputs on non-line like features by checking that the pixels brightness values have the correct type of relationship with one another to be part of a line segment.

Another problem that tends to occur with all feature detectors based on convolution masks is one of scale. For example, the line detector responds well to lines one pixel wide, but its output on a line 3 pixels wide is 0. The size of a line in an image depends only on the scale or magnification used by the image acquisition equipment. What is a 1-pixel wide line in one image can easily be changed into a 3-pixel wide line in another by increasing the magnification. The only successful approach to this problem is to use a number of feature detectors covering a range of scales. When this is added to the need to use a number of detectors to cover a range of orientations, the local feature detection task can involve examining the output of a great many operators for each feature.

The decision process — non-maxima suppression

Most local feature detectors output a value that indicates how likely it is that the feature exists at each point in the image. To take the next step and detect such features it is necessary to examine these values and decide at each point whether the feature is present or not. In most cases, this amounts to thresholding the resulting image. The main problem, in common with all thresholding procedures, is selecting an optimum threshold value. Usually, this is done empirically by examining the results from a sample of images. In the case of edge and line segments a high threshold is often used to extract the points which are most certainly parts of edges or lines and then further processing is applied to the image to find the points with the lower values which are also likely to be part of the same edges or lines by virtue of their position. (This type of method is described in Chapter Five.)

A characteristic of convolution mask detectors is that their output tends to be 'thick'. That is, a mask will give high outputs in a large region close to the target feature, as well as at the position of best fit. Local non-maxima suppression is a technique particularly suited to this problem. Put simply, this involves ignoring all points which are close to a point with a larger value. That is, if there is a larger value within some neighbourhood then the point's value can be set to 0. The only problem is selecting the size of the neighbourhood and this is most usefully taken to be the same as the size of the convolution mask in use.

The following subroutine will perform non-maxima suppression in a m% by n% window shifted into every position of the image in i%, storing the results back in i%.

```
SUB lms(i%(2),p%,q%,m%,n%) STATIC
FOR i%=0 TO p%-1
```

```
  FOR j%=0 TO q%-1
    max=i%(i%,j%)
    FOR k%=0 TO m%
      FOR l%=0 TO n%
        IF i%(i%+k%,j%+l%)>max THEN i%(i%,j%) =0
      NEXT l%
    NEXT k%
  NEXT j%
NEXT i%
END SUB
```

It is also worth noticing that line detectors based on the second derivative can be used without thresholding, since the presence of a line is indicated by a 'zero crossing', that is a change from a positive to a negative value. This idea is central to another approach to pattern recognition – *computational vision* (see the Further Reading section on page 138).

Chapter Four
The Frequency Approach

Earlier chapters have considered ways of processing grey level images directly – that is, the methods have concentrated on working with the grey level at each point of the picture. Such methods are usually referred to as *spatial methods*. An attractive alternative to the spatial method is that which examines the composition of the image in terms of the way it can be made up from a series of period functions. Such methods are usually referred to as *frequency methods*. This chapter looks at the use of the concept of transforming the image into a frequency representation and how this relates to the now familiar spatial methods introduced in Chapter Three. Some of the methods described in this chapter depend on the use of the Fourier transform and the Fourier series, and a prior knowledge of these topics is an advantage, although not essential, to a full appreciation of frequency-based methods.

Spatial frequency and the Fourier transform

Frequency is a term which is generally supposed to refer to the rate of repetition of some periodic event. In image processing, spatial frequency is essentially the rate at which the brightness of an image changes with distance. High spatial frequencies correspond to rapidly varying detail and low frequencies correspond to slowly changing brightness. For example, a sharp edge consists of high spatial frequencies but a large gently shaded region consists of low spatial frequencies.

It has long been known that it is possible to decompose any motion into a series of simple periodic motions of varying frequencies. The best known such decomposition is the *Fourier transform* which is based on the use of sine waves. For example, a square wave can be considered to be made up of a sum of sine waves of frequency 1f, 3f, 5f .... (where f is the frequency of the square wave):

64 *Pattern Recognition*

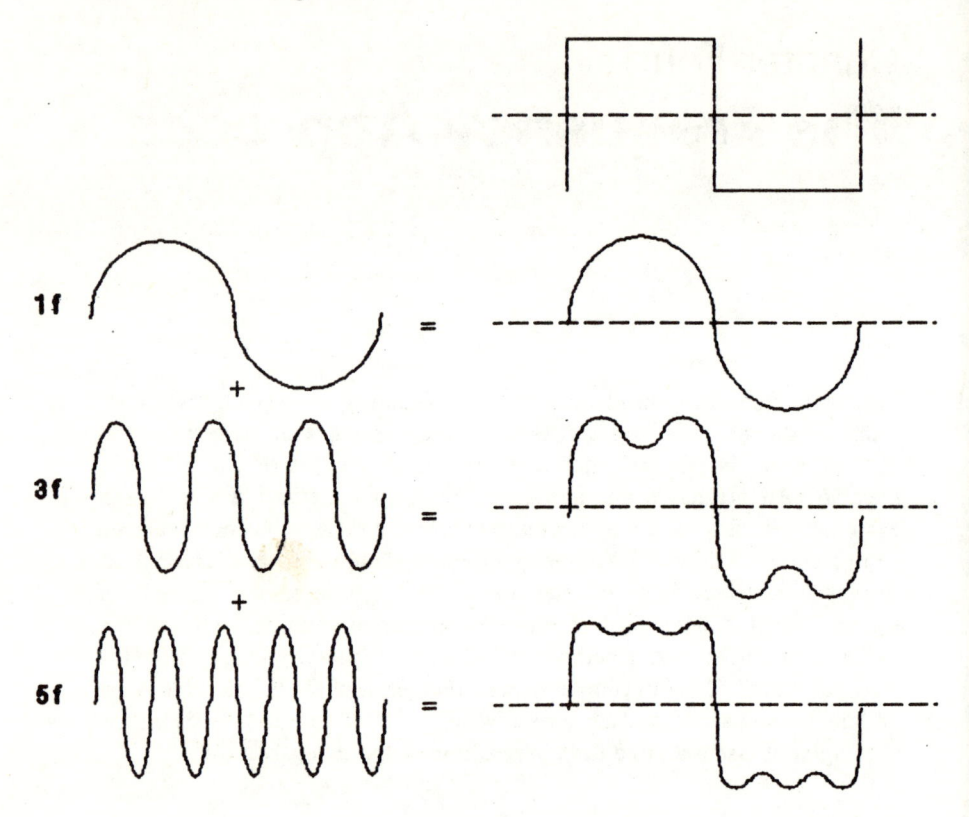

As the number of sine waves included in the sum increases, the resulting waveform looks more and more like an exact square wave.

In the same way any waveform can be thought of as being made up of a mixture of sine waves. A graph showing the decomposition of a waveform into its frequency components is called its *spectrum*. A complete spectrum specifies the amount of each frequency, its amplitude and how much the sine wave has to be shifted with respect to the others – its *phase*. The relationship between a waveform and its spectrum is two-way in the sense that given a waveform you can deduce its spectrum, and given a spectrum you can deduce its waveform. In this sense the spectrum is interchangeable with the waveform. The spectrum contains the same information as the waveform but in a different arrangement. However, this duality only holds when you consider the complete spectrum as containing information about the amplitude and the phase at each frequency (see Fig. 4.1).

Many applications use only the amplitude information, or the amplitude squared, and discard the phase information. It is argued that only the amount of each frequency in the image is important, not the relative phase of each

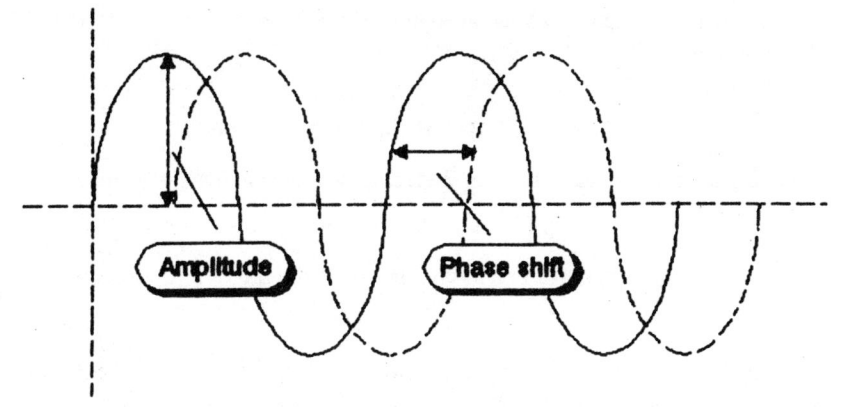

Fig. 4.1 Phase and amplitude

component. This is sometimes true, but it is important not to underestimate the amount of information contained in the phase part of the spectrum. A waveform (or image) reconstructed using only phase information is often surprisingly like the original. A graph of the square of the amplitude is known as the *power spectrum* of the waveform because the square of the amplitude is proportional to the power (i.e. to the energy) at the given frequency. The main reason for ignoring phase in plots of the spectrum of a waveform is that it is very difficult to interpret meaningfully, but it is vital to appreciate that without the additional phase information a waveform cannot be reconstructed.

The Fourier transform

The Fourier transform F(w) of a function f(x) is defined as:

$$F(w) = \int_{-\infty}^{+\infty} f(x)e^{-i2\pi wx}dx$$

It is important to realise that F(w) is a complex function which contains both amplitude and phase information. If a+ib is the value of F(w) at a particular frequency then a^2+b^2 is the amplitude squared (or power) and $\tan^{-1}(a/b)$ is the phase angle. The inverse Fourier transform is:

$$f(x) = \int_{-\infty}^{+\infty} F(w)e^{i2\pi wx}dw$$

To avoid having to write integral signs the Fourier transform of a function can be written FT(f(x)), that is F(w)=FT(f(x)).

The Fourier transform is linear:

$$FT[af(x)+bg(x)] = aFT(f(x)) + bFT(g(x))$$

Changing the spatial scale changes the frequency scale in inverse proportion:

$$FT(f(ax)) = 1/aF(w/a)$$

and a shift of the function's origin changes only the phase of the spectrum:

$$FT(f(x-a)) = F(w)e^{i2piwa}$$

Surprisingly, it is this last property which has often made the Fourier transform attractive from the point of view of image processing. If the only effect that shifting an image has on its Fourier transform is to alter the phase information then the amplitude or power spectrum is invariant to such a shift. Thus, it should be possible to use the power spectrum of an image to recognise it irrespective of any shifts to which it may be subject, without having to go to the trouble of convolving a mask with it. That is, the power spectrum of a letter A is always the same, no matter where it is positioned on the page.

The Fourier transform of an image is, of course, a two-dimensional affair given by:

$$F(w,v) = \int_{-\infty}^{+\infty} \int_{-\infty}^{+\infty} f(x,y) e^{-i2\pi(wx+vy)} dx\, dy$$

Fortunately this complicated integral can be performed as two separate one-dimensional integrals which correspond exactly to the usual one-dimensional Fourier transform – that is the two-dimensional Fourier transform is *separable*.

$$F(w,y) = \int_{-\infty}^{+\infty} f(x,y) e^{-i2\pi wx} dx$$

$$F(w,v) = \int_{-\infty}^{+\infty} F(w,y) e^{-i2\pi vy} dy$$

The discrete Fourier Transform

The usual theory of the Fourier transform applies to functions defined on a continuous interval, but the images which are processed by computer are defined on a discrete set of points a_{ij}. As you might expect, there is a corresponding theory involving the use of the *discrete Fourier transform* which applies in this case. The discrete Fourier transform of a set of n values a_i, i=1, 2, ..., n is obtained by simply replacing the integral sign in the definition of the Fourier transform by a summation giving:

$$w_k = \sum_{i=0}^{n-1} a_i e^{-i2\pi ki/n}$$

k=0,1,2,...n−1

$$a_i = \frac{1}{n} \sum_{k=0}^{n-1} w_k e^{i2\pi ki/n}$$

k=0,1,2,...n−1

The discrete Fourier transform can be easily written in matrix form:

$W = e^{-i2\pi/n}$

$$F = \begin{bmatrix} 1 & 1 & 1 & ..1 \\ 1 & W & W^2 & W^{n-1} \\ 1 & W^2 & W^4 & W^{2(n-1)} \\ 1 & W^3 & W^6 & W^{3(n-1)} \\ 1 & W^4 & W^8 & W^{4(n-1)} \\ 1 & W^{(n-1)} & W^{2(n-1)} & ..W^{(n-1)(n-1)} \end{bmatrix}$$

w = Fa

The two-dimensional discrete Fourier transform is separable and can be computed by first taking the discrete Fourier transform of the rows, and then taking the discrete Fourier transform of the columns of the result.

The discrete Fourier transform of n values produces n complex numbers. As a complex number, z is equivalent to a pair of real numbers, i.e. z=a+ib, and it appears that the Fourier transform has spread the information in the image into twice as many numbers. In fact, the Fourier transform of a real image (or function) is symmetrical about the n/2 term, so there are only n independent real values in the Fourier transform.

The fast Fourier transform

To calculate the discrete Fourier transform directly using the equation given earlier is very time-consuming – taking n^2 complex multiplications and n^2 complex additions to transform n values. The discovery of a method, the *fast Fourier transform* (FFT), of calculating the Fourier transform in only $n\log_2 n$ multiplications has made it possible to compute the two-dimensional Fourier

(a) Original image of tartan cloth and label

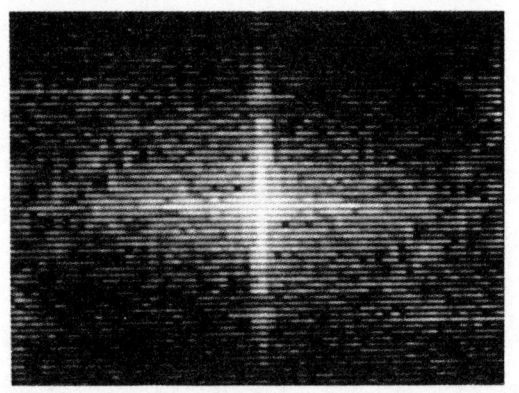

(b) Fourier transform of (a) in optical form. Notice the strong horizontal and vertical frequency components corresponding to the tartan pattern

(c) Original image of cloth rotated through 45°

Plate 5 Examples of two-dimensional Fourier transform

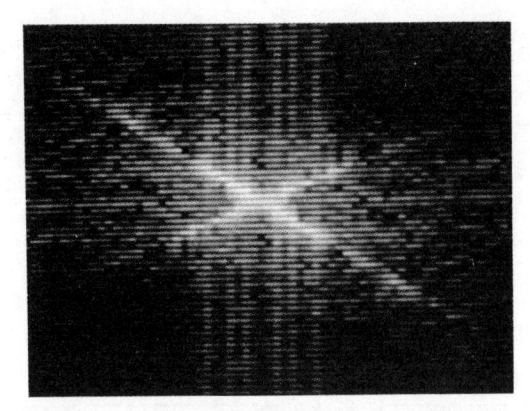

(d) Fourier transform of (c). Notice that the strong horizontal and vertical frequency components have rotated by 45°. What do you think causes the remaining horizontal and vertical components?

Plate 5   Examples of two-dimensional Fourier transform

transform of fairly large grey level images in a time that would have been unattainable only a few years ago. As the FFT is simply a faster way of calculating the discrete Fourier transform, there is no real need to understand the principles which lie behind it in order to use the Fourier transform in image processing, although they are interesting in their own right.

The discrete Fourier transform can be written as:

$$w_k = \sum_{i=0}^{n-1} a_i W_n^{ki}$$

$$k=0,1,2,\ldots n-1$$

where:
$$W_n = e^{-i2\pi/n}$$

A great saving in computation can be achieved by writing the sum separately for the even and odd values of the index i. That is:

Even $\qquad\qquad$ **Odd**

$$w_k = \sum_{i=0}^{n/2-1} a_{2i} W_n^{2ki} \quad + \quad \sum_{i=0}^{n/2-1} a_{2i+1} W_n^{k(2i+1)}$$

and as:
$$W_n^2 = W_{n/2}$$

$$w_k = \sum_{i=0}^{n/2-1} a_{2i} W_{n/2}^{ki} \quad + \quad W_n^k \sum_{i=0}^{n/2-1} a_{2i+1} W_{n/2}^{ki}$$

which gives for: $k \leqslant n/2 - 1$

$$w_k = FT_k(\text{even}) + W_n^k FT_k(\text{odd})$$

and for: $k > n/2-1$

$$w_k = FT_{k-n/2}(\text{even}) - W_n^{k-n/2} FT_{k-n/2}(\text{odd})$$

Where FT_k(even) and FT_k(odd) are the kth element of the n/2 Fourier transforms of the even and odd elements of a respectively.

This gives rise to the following scheme for computing, say, an eight-value discrete Fourier transform:

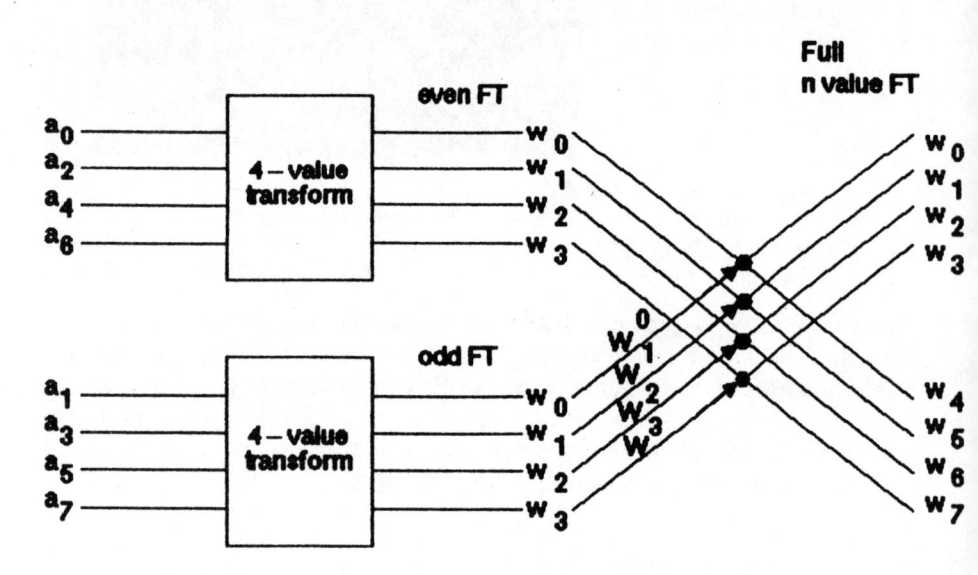

The division into two series can be repeated on the four-value transforms giving a pair of two-value transforms. In general, for an n-value transform, where n is a power of two, the discrete Fourier transform can be broken down until a two-value transform is all that is needed. Computing the discrete Fourier transform in this way reduces the number of multiplications needed to $n\log_2 n$ which for even moderate n is considerably smaller than n^2.

A subroutine for the two-dimensional FFT

The following subroutines implement a two-dimensional FFT. Rather than being highly optimised, the subroutines are organised to show the principles of the FFT. The first subroutine takes the one-dimensional FFT of the data stored in the one-dimensional arrays rd(real part) and id (imaginary part); both arrays have n% elements which must be a power of 2, for example, 16, 32, 64 etc. If isi% is −1 then the FFT is computed. If isi% is +1 then the inverse FFT is computed. The results are calculated 'in place' and so are returned in rd and id. An important point to notice is that the data is stored starting at rd(1) and id(1) which is different from the convention used for images which are stored starting with the zeroth element.

```
SUB fft(rd(1),id(1),n%,isi%) STATIC
      REM routine by C. M. Rader, MIT Lincoln Lab
      REM data in bit-reversed order
      j%=1
      FOR i%=1 TO n%
       IF i%<j% THEN call exch(rd(),id(),n%,i%,j%)
       m%=n%/2
       WHILE j%>m%
         j%=j%-m%
         m%=int((m%+1)/2)
       WEND
       j%=j%+m%
      NEXT i%
      REM compute the butterflies
      mmax%=1
      WHILE mmax%<n%
       istep%=2*mmax%
       FOR m%=1 TO mmax%
         theta=3.1415*csng(isi%)
          *csng(m%-1)/csng(mmax%)
         wr=cos(theta)
         wi=sin(theta)
         FOR i%=m% to n% STEP istep%
           j%=i%+mmax%
           tempr=wr*rd(j%)-wi*id(j%)
           tempi=wr*id(j%)+wi*rd(j%)
           rd(j%)=rd(i%)-tempr
           id(j%)=id(i%)-tempi
           rd(i%)=rd(i%)+tempr
           id(i%)=id(i%)+tempi
         NEXT i%
       NEXT m%
       mmax%=istep%
      WEND
      IF isi%=-1 THEN EXIT SUB
      FOR i%=1 TO n%
       rd(i%)=rd(i%)/n%
       id(i%)=id(i%)/n%
      NEXT i%
END SUB
SUB exch(rd(1),id(1),n%,i%,j%) STATIC
      temp=rd(i%)
      rd(i%)=rd(j%)
      rd(j%)=temp
      temp=id(i%)
      id(i%)=id(j%)
      id(j%)=temp
END SUB
```

Once you have a one-dimensional FFT, taking the two-dimensional FFT of an image stored in an array is just a matter of taking the transform of each of the rows followed by the transform of each of the columns. The following subroutine does just this by transferring the rows of the image, stored in jr (real part) and ji(imaginary part) one at a time into the one-dimensional arrays rd and id, and then calling the one-dimensional FFT subroutine given above. The results of the one-dimensional FFT are stored back into the same rows from which the original data was taken. After all the rows have been transformed the procedure is repeated, but using the columns. The two-dimensional arrays are nn% by nn% and the one-dimensional arrays are nn%. If isi% is −1, the FFT is calculated. If isi% is +1, the inverse FFT is calculated. Notice that usually for a grey level image, the imaginary part, stored in ji, has to be set to 0. The data should be stored in the two-dimensional arrays starting from jr(0,0) and ji(0,0). The result of the transform or inverse transform is returned in the same arrays with the DC or 0 frequency component stored in jr(0,0) and ji(0,0). This subroutine takes about eight minutes to process a 64 × 64 image using an IBM PC and Quick BASIC.

```
SUB fft2d (jr(2),ji(2),rd(1),id(1),nn%,isi%) STATIC
REM fast fourier tranform
REM put rows into single-dimension array
REM and call fourier subroutine
    FOR j%=1 TO nn%
     FOR i%=1 TO nn%
      rd(i%)=jr(i%-1,j%-1)
      id(i%)=ji(i%-1,j%-1)
     NEXT i%
     CALL fft(rd(),id(),nn%,isi%)
     FOR i%=1 TO nn%
      jr(i%-1,j%-1)=rd(i%)
      ji(i%-1,j%-1)=id(i%)
     NEXT i%
    NEXT j%
REM put cols into single-dimension array
REM and call fourier subroutine
    FOR i%=1 TO nn%
     FOR j%=1 TO nn%
      rd(j%)=jr(i%-1,j%-1)
      id(j%)=ji(i%-1,j%-1)
     NEXT j%
     CALL fft(rd(),id(),nn%,isi%)
     FOR j%=1 TO nn%
      jr(i%-1,j%-1)=rd(j%)
      ji(i%-1,j%-1)=id(j%)
```

```
    NEXT j%
  NEXT i%
END SUB
```

To convert the results of the FFT from complex numbers to something that can be displayed it is necessary to take the magnitude of each value. The following subroutine calculates the magnitude of the complex number pair stored in jr(i,j) and ji(i,j) and stores the result in jr(i,j). To compress the range of values to make it more suitable for display, it is the log of the magnitude that is actually calculated.

```
SUB power(jr(2),ji(2),nn%) STATIC
    FOR i%=0 TO nn%-1
      FOR j%=0 TO nn%-1
        jr(i%,j%)=jr(i%,j%)*jr(i%,j%)
           +ji(i%,j%)*ji(i%,j%)
        IF jr(i%,j%)>0 THEN jr(i%,j%)=log(jr(i%,j%))
      NEXT j%
    NEXT i%
END SUB
```

Before displaying the result of this subroutine it is usually necessary to convert the real numbers to integers and scale the output to lie within the range of grey levels that the display can cope with.

Sampling effects

The discrete Fourier transform of a digital image is usually regarded as an approximation to the Fourier transform of the continuous image from which the digital image was obtained. This approximation is subject to a number of important effects caused by the nature of the sampling process. The first effect is due to the presence of extra edge caused by the image border. The discrete Fourier transform assumes that the digital image is just one period of an infinite periodic function and, if the values at the opposite edges of the function are not the same, the result is additional edge discontinuities (see Fig. 4.2).

Edge discontinuities introduce spurious frequencies into the spectrum when compared with the spectrum of the non-periodic continuous function. In other words, the discrete Fourier transform accurately represents the spectrum of the function within the sampling window, but not that of the Fourier transform of the continuous function from which it was obtained. These extra frequencies may or may not be troublesome, depending on the purpose to which the spectrum is to be put. If they are troublesome, they can be reduced by smoothing the image down to 0 towards its edges, so producing 'soft' rather than 'hard' edges.

74 *Pattern Recognition*

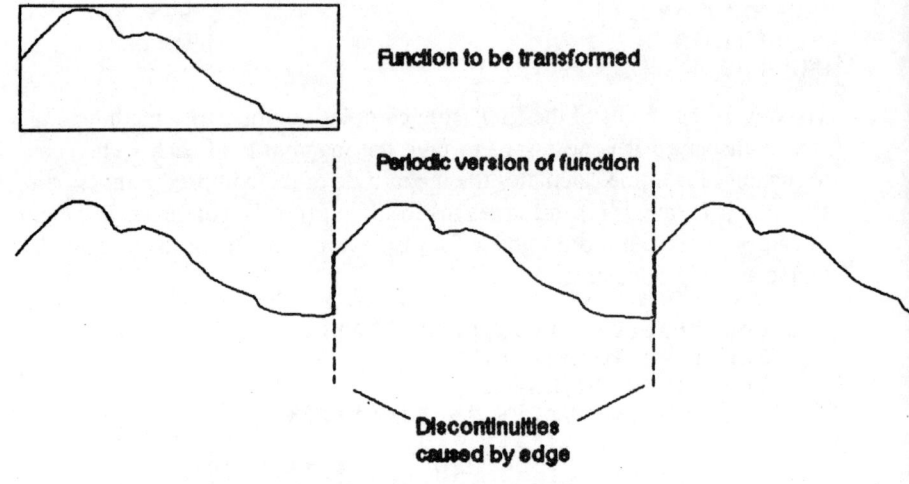

Fig. 4.2   Edge discontinuities

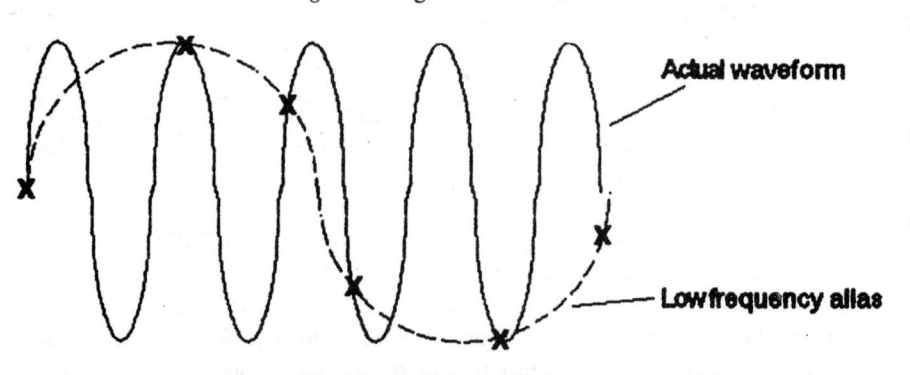

Fig. 4.3   Frequency aliasing

Perhaps the most important source of inaccuracy is due to under sampling which causes *frequency aliasing*. A high frequency sine wave sampled at too low a rate is indistinguishable from the samples that would be obtained from a lower frequency sine wave (see Fig. 4.3).

Thus under sampling causes high frequency components in the original image to be mistaken for low frequency components in the digitised image. The high frequency is said to be *aliased* with the low frequency. The solution to this problem is to sample the original image twice in each cycle of the highest frequency it contains – this sampling rate is called the *Nyquist frequency*. Of course, in practice the highest frequency an image contains isn't known exactly, and either a theoretical upper limit is used or the image is low pass filtered (see below for details of filtering) to impose a limit.

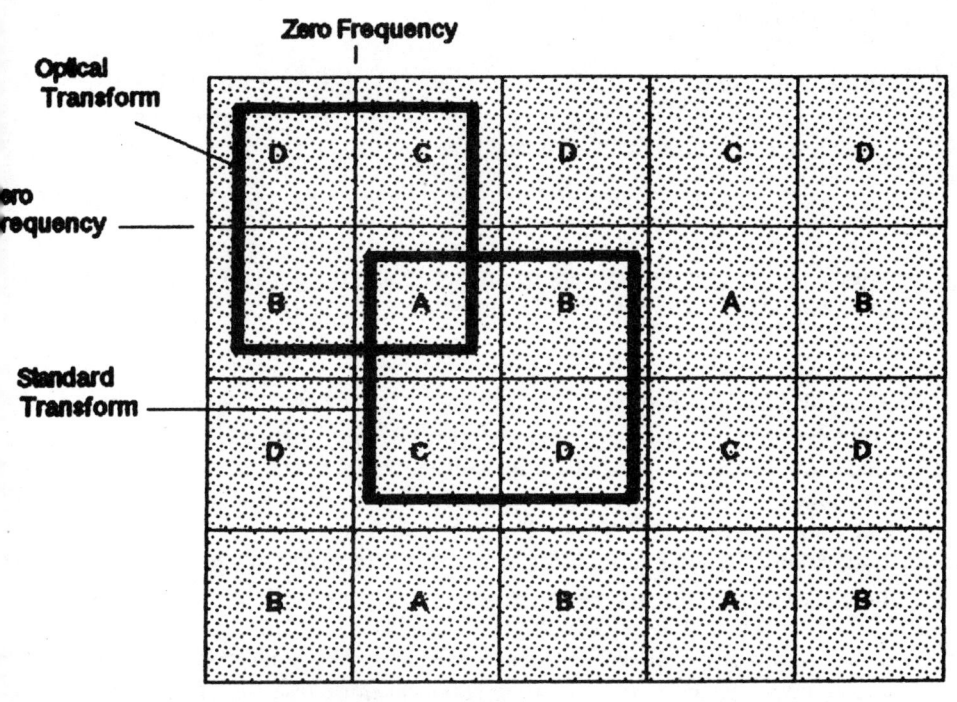

Fig. 4.4 Optical and standard forms of the Fourier transform

Standard and optical transforms

The standard form of the Fourier transform produces a spectrum with the zero frequency component in the top left-hand corner. A more familiar form of display places the zero frequency component in the centre of the display. This difference doesn't cause any problems because the Fourier transform is both symmetric and periodic, and placing the zero frequency component in the middle can be achieved by a simple rearrangement as shown in Fig. 4.4.

The form of the Fourier transform with the zero frequency component at the centre of the display is usually referred to as the *optical form* because this is the way that it is naturally produced by some optical methods of generating it. It can be shown that the optical form can be produced by multiplying each value of the image by $(-1)^{(i+j)}$ where i and j are the line and column indices. Another problem with displaying the spectrum is that the zero frequency component is typically very much larger than the other components and swamps any detail in the rest of the spectrum. To overcome this problem, the zero frequency component is often left out of any displays by setting it to 0 or by plotting the log of the values (see the listing of subroutine power given above).

The convolution theorem

So far we have not examined any of the practical uses of the Fourier transform. One of the most important of these is in computing the convolution of a mask with an image. The *convolution theorem* states that:

$$FT(f*g)=FT(f)FT(g)$$

where f*g signifies the convolution of f and g. That is, the convolution of two images can be computed by multiplying the Fourier transforms of each image and then taking the inverse Fourier transform:

$$f*g = FT^{-1}(FT(f)FT(g))$$

Using the fast Fourier transform is a much faster way of computing the convolution of a mask with an image (see Chapter Three). However, it is important to recall this slight complication: the mathematical operation of convolution is defined in such a way that it corresponds to the masking operation described in Chapter Three, but with the mask reversed top to bottom and left to right. This difference is usually ignored in image processing because most masks are symmetric, in which case $g(x)=g(-x)$ and both definitions of convolution give the same results.

If a normalised convolution is required, the mask should be normalised before taking its Fourier transform. The local normalisation of the image cannot be achieved before or during the Fourier transform. The only way that this can be achieved is by dividing the results of the convolution by the local standard deviation computed in a region the same size as the mask.

Filtering

Multiplying each point of the Fourier transform of an image by a weighting function to enhance or reduce each frequency component before performing the inverse transform is referred to as *filtering*. That is, if F(w) is the Fourier transform of the image f(x) i.e. F=FT(f), and G(w) is a filter, then h(x) given by:

$$h(x) = FT^{-1}[F(w)G(w)]$$

is the result of filtering F with G. Using the convolution theorem it is obvious that:

$$\begin{aligned} h(x) &= FT^{-1}[F(w)G(w)] \\ &= FT^{-1}[FT(f(x))FT(g(x))] \\ &= f(x)*g(x) \end{aligned}$$

where G(w)=FT(g(x)). That is, filtering is equivalent to convolution, and it is simply the frequency and spatial form of the same operation.

Filters are generally used to compensate for defects, usually of known origin, in the image. For example, a *high pass filter* stops all frequencies above a certain cut-off value and can be used to remove high frequency noise. Similarly a *low pass filter*, stops all frequencies below a cut-off value, and can be used to remove low frequency noise. A *band pass filter* or *band stop filter* passes or stops a range of frequencies and can be used to remove periodic noise of a known frequency. An isotropic band pass (or band stop) filter treats all frequencies the same irrespective of their direction, and takes the form of an anular region, as shown in Figure 4.5.

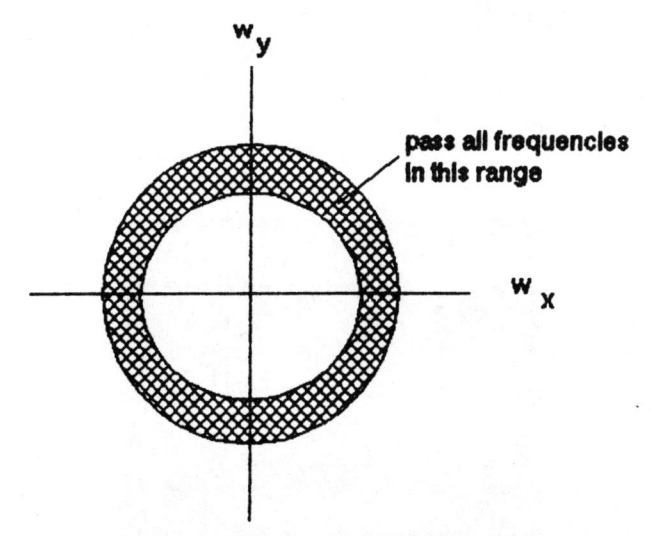

Fig. 4.5 An isotropic two-dimensional band pass filter

Convolution masks are generally used when searching for local features because they are easier to design than their corresponding filter. Of course, the masking operation may be implemented as an equivalent filtering operation, but it is the mask which plays the important conceptual role and the filter is just a convenient and efficient way of implementing the operation. Filters are mainly used for image restoration or enhancement where they are more directly connected with the nature of the problem. There are two distinct ways in which they are used – subjective enhancement and analytical enhancement. Subjective enhancement proceeds by displaying the spectrum of an image and asking an operator which frequencies should be suppressed. Typically the operator will be able to identify a number of bright spots in the spectrum which correspond to the frequencies introduced into the image by the noise

78 Pattern Recognition

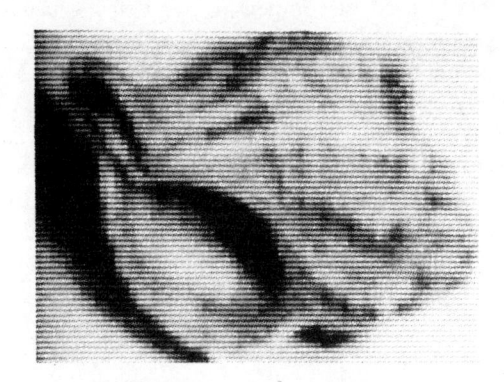

(a) Original image of a shell

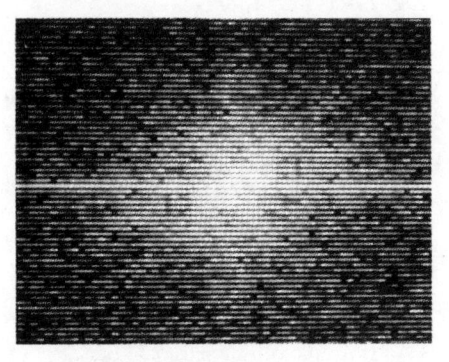

(b) Fourier transform of (a) in optical form

Plate 6 An example of filtering

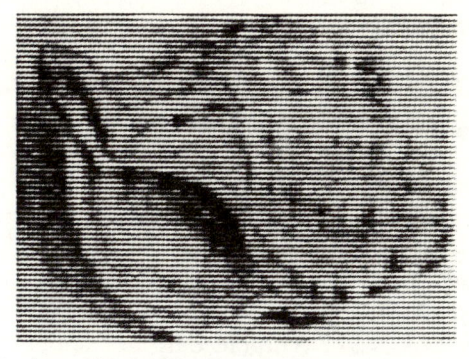

(c) High pass filtering of (a). Notice that the shell markings are sharper

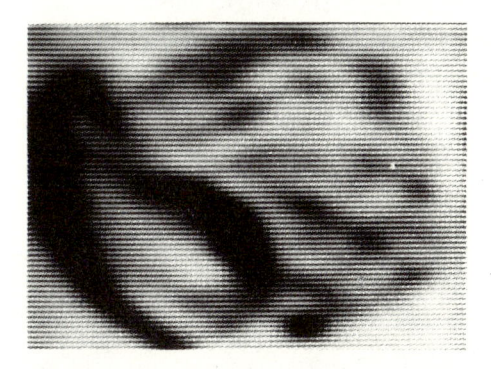

(d) Low pass filtering. The image is very blurred

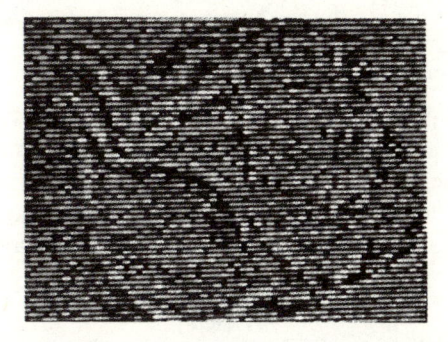

(e) The result of a phase filter. As all amplitude information has been lost and the reconstructed image only uses the phase information it is remarkable that the shape of the shell can be seen at all

that degraded it. This is an interactive and iterative process in that the image is displayed along with its spectrum and an operator attempts to construct a filter which will result in an acceptable image.

The alternative, and more traditional, method of constructing a filter uses a model of the process that degraded the image to deduce an optimal filter that removes the degradation. Optimal filter design can be highly mathematical and would lead us into some difficult areas. However, simple filtering to remove noise with known statistical properties is straightforward enough. If the original image $f(x,y)$ has been degraded by the addition of random noise $n(x,y)$ with known statistical properties (e.g. it is normally distributed), the image in question is given by:

$$g(x,y) = f(x,y) + n(x,y)$$

Usually an image will also be degraded by the effect of the image acquisition system which can normally be described as a convolution of the image with a function $h(x,y)$ which is called the *systems impulse response* function. Thus, a more general model of image degradation is given by:

$$g(x,y) = h(x,y)*f(x,y)+n(x,y)$$

and the objective in filtering $g(x,y)$ is to recover as nearly as possible the image $f(x,y)$. Taking the Fourier transform gives:

$$FT(g(x,y)) = FT(h(x,y)FT(f(x,y) + FT(n(x,y))$$

or

$$G(w,v) = H(w,v)F(w,v) + N(w,v)$$

The most obvious way to recover $f(x,y)$ is to solve the above equation for F and then take its inverse Fourier transform, that is:

$$F(w,v) = \frac{G(w,v) - N(w,v)}{H(w,v)}$$

The trouble with this simple method is that $N(w,v)$ is rarely known exactly and $H(w,v)$ often vanishes or becomes very small for some values of w,v. There are a number of ways around this problem. Most are based on an attempt to find a filter which will give the best approximation to $F(w,v)$. For example, the *Wiener filter*, $W(w,v)$, gives a least squares approximation to $F(w,v)$:

$$W(w,v) = \frac{H^*(w,v)}{|H(w,v)|^2 + S_n(w,v)/S_f(w,v)}$$

and:

$$F(w,v) = W(w,v)G(w,v)$$

The Frequency Approach 81

where H*(w,v) is the complex conjugate of H(w,v), |H(w,v)| is its amplitude, $S_n(w,v)$ and $S_f(w,v)$ are the *spectral densities* of the noise and the image respectively. The spectral density is, roughly speaking, a spectrum averaged over all the images under consideration. If $S_n(w,v)$ and $S_f(w,v)$ are not known, a common procedure is to assume a constant ratio which is adjusted to obtain good results.

Other transformations

The Fourier transformation is just one of a large class of linear orthogonal transformations which can be used in image processing. The best known of these is the *Hadamard transform*, which decomposes a function or an image into a sum of rectangular waveforms. The Hadamard transform, and most of the other alternatives to the Fourier transform, offer the advantage of being quick to compute, but they lack the natural interpretation in terms of frequency spectrum which makes the Fourier transform so easy to work with. Most image processing applications of these alternatives to the Fourier transform are used for data compression rather than analysis or recognition.

Fourier features

One of the least obvious applications of the Fourier transform is using the frequency components themselves as features – *Fourier features* – in a classification rule. This idea arises because, ignoring phase changes, the Fourier transform is independent of the position of the image, i.e. it is invariant to shifts. This suggests that using the values of the frequency components in a classification rule should produce a shift invariant rule. There is also an argument that most of the information in an image is contained in the lower frequency components because the high frequency components are concerned with the fine detail of the image. Thus, in principle, it should be possible to construct a classification rule which performs well using only a few Fourier features. There is no claim to any sort of optimality in the use of Fourier features – indeed, it is known that there are alternative transformations, the *Karhunen-Loeve transformation* or the *singular value decomposition* (SVD) for example, which give better results than the Fourier transform, but they are much more time-consuming to calculate. Notice that the use of Fourier features is not an attempt to construct a local feature detector. Components of the spectrum of the entire image are used to classify the entire image.

For example, you might have a set of images of letters of the alphabet such that each image contained just one letter. The Fourier feature approach to classifying them would compute the spectrum of each image and use the frequency components in a classification rule. In general, it is better to use features based on the presence or absence of local features.

Spatial v frequency methods – removing noise

Almost all image processing can be tackled from either a spatial or a frequency analysis point of view. This is a simple consequence of the fact that a Fourier transform of an image contains as much information as the original image and of the correspondence between filtering and convolution. Which point of view leads to the simplest or most effective solution depends very much on the nature of the problem. For example, if we are trying to remove *salt and pepper* noise, that is, isolated bright and dark points, from an image, the spatial point of view is probably better. The reason for this is that we have a local model for the pattern of grey levels which define the pixel value that we would like to modify. To remove salt and pepper noise using a spatial operation we could employ any sort of local smoothing. If this local smoothing is implemented as a convolution, clearly there is an equivalent low pass filter, but the advantage of considering the problem in spatial terms is that it suggests simple but non-linear smoothing techniques which do not correspond to filtering. For example, as we are trying to remove points which are very different from their neighbours, we could use *median smoothing* (sometimes confusingly referred to as 'median filtering' even though it does not correspond to a simple filter). Median smoothing involves replacing every pixel by the *median* value of its neighbours. The median of a set of numbers is a value such that 50% are larger and 50% are smaller, that is, it is the middle value. A median filter is difficult to implement but it is very effective at removing salt and pepper noise without blurring edges.

As an example of a problem best tackled from the frequency point of view, consider the task of removing noise in the form of *hum bars*. Most electronic equipment tends to pick up 50 Hz interference from the mains, and in video equipment this tends to appear as regular light and dark bars across the image, hence the name 'hum bars'. To remove hum bars using a local operation is clearly difficult, but a filter is very easy to construct. To remove hum bars all that is necessary is a 50 Hz band stop filter, that is, a filter that removes frequencies close to 50 Hz.

The main difference between the spatial approach and the frequency approach to problems is that the spatial viewpoint seems to favour problems with local structure and the frequency viewpoint seems to favour problems with global or period structure. It is important to be familiar and comfortable with both points of view for a full understanding of many image processing methods.

Chapter Five
Grey Level Features – II Segmentation

In Chapter Three the idea of a local feature and how to detect it was introduced. An alternative approach to image classification attempts to divide the image up into regions based on some property or another. In many ways these two approaches are complementary and this chapter examines the methods and techniques of image segmentation.

Segmentation as pixel classification

Given an image, the task of dividing it into similar regions can be thought of as classifying each pixel in the image into one of a number of types. For example, a simple threshold may result in the division of the pixels in an image into a foreground object and the background. However, most segmentation schemes are much more complicated than this. *Region growing* is a technique where an initial classification is made, and then the resulting groups of pixels are examined to see if the classification could be improved by merging any of the groups.

For example, a line segment detector could be used to identify groups of pixels which belong to a line. This is the initial classification. Based on this, the pixels between the line segments already identified could be examined to see if they are likely candidates for addition to a larger line segment and so on. Thus, region growing is often an iterative process – each reallocation of pixels reduces the likelihood of other pixels belonging to the region.

An alternative approach is *region splitting* where a larger region is divided into smaller and smaller regions depending on finer and finer distinctions between the properties of the pixels. Whatever method is used, it is helpful to think of the purpose of segmentation being to provide each pixel with a label indicating the type of region to which it belongs. This can be clearly seen as an extension of the binary predicate function introduced in Chapter One as a way of labelling the pixels as either background or foreground.

Regions and boundaries

It is clear that edge detection can be used to extract regions from an image. Given a sufficiently good detector, sensitive to the change between different regions of the image, it should be possible to extract the region within the closed boundary produced by the edge detector. In practice, edge detectors are not good enough to guarantee a connected boundary surrounding a region and further processing is necessary to fill in the gaps. On the other hand, a region always specifies a closed boundary and this is one of the main attractions of the segmentation approach.

Segmentation by thresholding

Thresholding was introduced in Chapter One as a method of separating a foreground object from the background. A fixed threshold simply assigns a value of 0 to a pixel if it less than the threshold and 1 otherwise. That is:

$$a_{ij} = 0 \text{ if } b_{ij} < 0$$
$$= 1 \text{ otherwise}$$

As mentioned in Chapter One, thresholding is not a particularly successful segmentation method unless special lighting is used. This has to be contrast enhancing and carefully controlled to provide even illumination for both the background and foreground objects.

Even a fixed threshold, the simplest of segmentation schemes, presents us with a problem in the choice of threshold to be used. For image enhancement purposes, the threshold can be chosen manually and this does indeed tend to produce the best results. However, it is important to realise that setting the threshold manually brings one of the best image processing computers – the brain – into the segmentation process, and any results obtained by processing the resulting thresholded image will depend on the high quality of the manual threshold setting. The best known method of automatic threshold setting is the histogram method described in Chapter One. Essentially, the threshold is chosen to lie in the valley, if there is one, of the image brightness histogram.

In practice, a fixed threshold usually cannot separate object from background because of the shading effects of the illumination, which makes some parts of the object darker than some parts of the background. There are two possible solutions to this type of problem - *multiple* and *variable* thresholds. A two-valued threshold assumes that the object pixels are generally greater than t_1 and background pixels generally less than t_2. On this assumption pixels greater than t_1 are classified as object, those less than t_2 are classified as background and those between t_1 and t_2 are unclassified. The

86 Pattern Recognition

unclassified pixels are then assigned to either object or background, depending on the class of the majority of their neighbours. A variable threshold assumes that in any given local region, pixels belonging to the object will have high brightness values compared to the local mean, and background points will have low brightness values compared to the local mean. Of course, to make the method work, you have to decide what size of area to consider and what constitutes high and low values with respect to the mean. One technique is to set the threshold t_{ij} to:

$$t_{ij} = k\, s(i,j) + m(i,j)$$

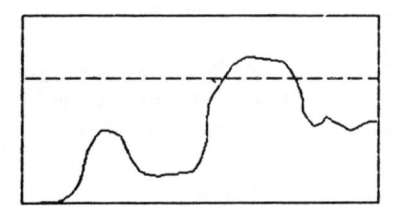

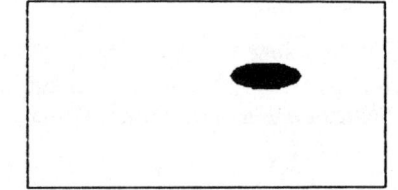

Fixed threshold set high extracts only one blob

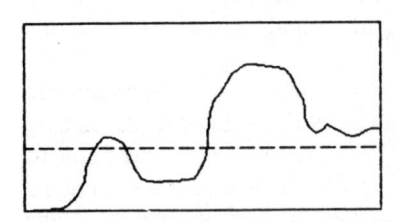

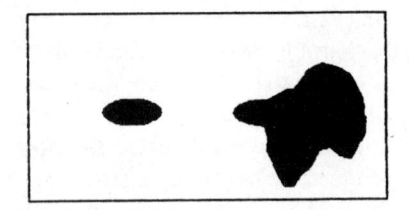

Fixed threshold set low extracts both blobs but with a lot of excess background

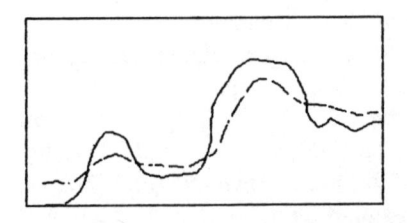

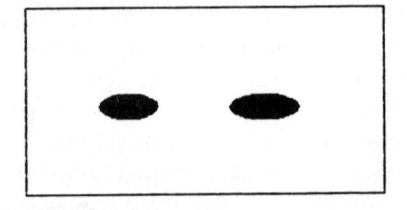

Variable threshold extracts both blobs without excess background

Fig. 5.1   Fixed and variable thresholding

where k is a constant, $s(i,j)$ is the local standard deviation and $m(i,j)$ is the local mean. The reason for including the standard deviation is that the higher the standard deviation the more the likelihood of the local region including both background and foreground pixels.

Smoothing

Thresholding and other segmentation methods can generally be improved by smoothing the image to remove noise and fine detail that will produce ragged or broken regions. The simplest smoothing method is to replace each pixel value by the average brightness within a small area surrounding it. This is often referred to as a *moving average* operation, but you should be able to see that it is nothing more than a standard convolution of the image with a mask. For example, if the local region is defined as a 3 × 3 area, the average can be computed by convolving the image with the mask:

$\frac{1}{9}$	$\frac{1}{9}$	$\frac{1}{9}$
$\frac{1}{9}$	$\frac{1}{9}$	$\frac{1}{9}$
$\frac{1}{9}$	$\frac{1}{9}$	$\frac{1}{9}$

As averaging corresponds to a convolution operation it can also be viewed as a filtering operation. Indeed, it is not difficult to show that smoothing operations based on averages correspond to low pass filtering (in the same way that edge detectors and 'sharpening' operations correspond to high pass filters) – see Chapter Four. The ideal smoothing operation would consolidate similar regions within the image but without blurring its edges. All low pass filters, and hence averaging operations, blur edges to some extent but some improvement can be obtained by using a weighted average with the weights decreasing toward the edges of the mask. For example:

$\frac{1}{16}$	$\frac{1}{8}$	$\frac{1}{16}$
$\frac{1}{8}$	$\frac{1}{4}$	$\frac{1}{8}$
$\frac{1}{16}$	$\frac{1}{8}$	$\frac{1}{16}$

There are a great many *ad hoc* smoothing operations which are not based on averaging and hence are not implementable as filters. The performance of these so called *non-linear* operators is difficult to assess theoretically but many do seem to perform well. They are all based on the idea that to smooth an image, pixels that are close and similar to one another should be made even more alike – that is, the application of a principle of *homogeneity*. For example, we could find the largest region surrounding each pixel that consisted of similar values and then apply a smoothing filter to just this region. (For another example see the description of the median filter at the end of Chapter Four.) All smoothing operations can be iterated to provided additional smoothing.

Regions from edges – line and curve detection

One of the reasons for attempting to find edges (or lines) in an image is to locate region boundaries and hence segment the image. The main problem with this is that edge detectors find edge segments and these tend not to be connected to form closed boundaries. Further processing has to be applied to the output of an edge detector in an attempt to form closed boundaries or a least larger boundary segments. Linking edge segments can be achieved by 'growing' the individual segments in a direction at right angles to the local gradient until they meet (see Fig. 5.2).

Once edge segments start to meet they will tend to form closed boundaries and the image can then be processed to remove remaining edge segments which do not form closed boundaries or form closed boundaries which are too small or too erratic. This algorithm is easy to describe and seems to correspond to what humans do when looking at the output of an edge detector, but it is remarkably difficult to implement efficiently.

One approach to finding edge segments which are part of the same straight edge is to use the Hough transform to detect collinear points. The general equation of a straight line is:

$$r = x \cos t + y \sin t$$

where t defines a direction at right angles to the line and r gives its distance from the origin (see Fig. 5.3).

If you consider a single point at x_i y_i then all the lines passing through it are obtained by varying r and t subject to the condition that:

$$x_i \cos t + y_i \sin t = r$$

If we consider r and t as new variables, the point x_i y_i corresponds to a curve in r t space called its *Hough transform* (see Fig. 5.4).

Grey Level Features – II **89**

Line segments   **Extended line segments**

Closed boundary

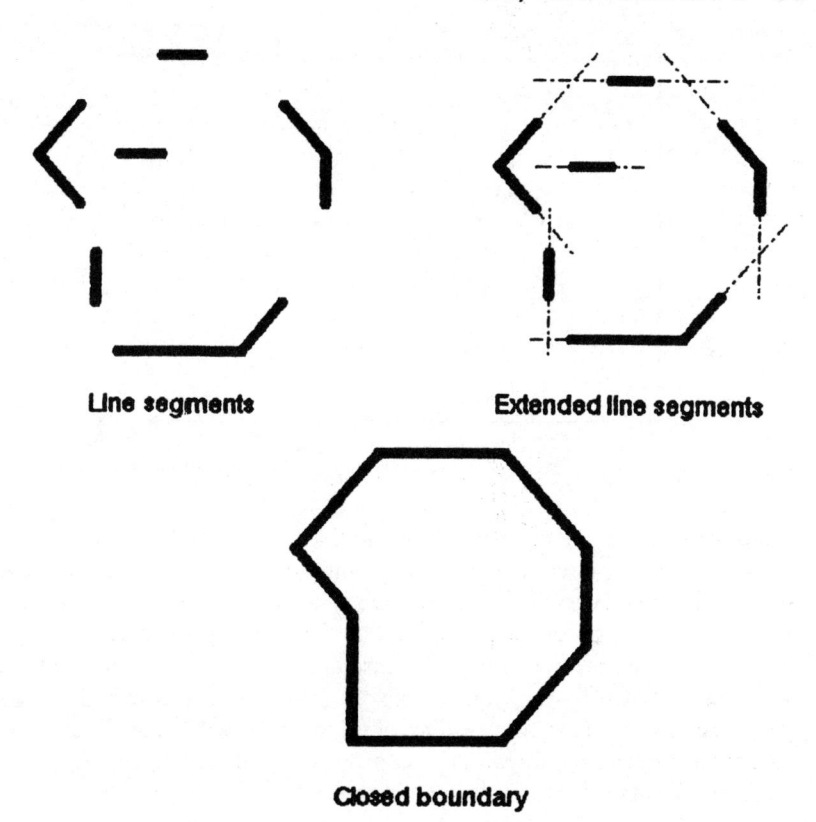

Fig. 5.2 Growing line segments to form a closed boundary

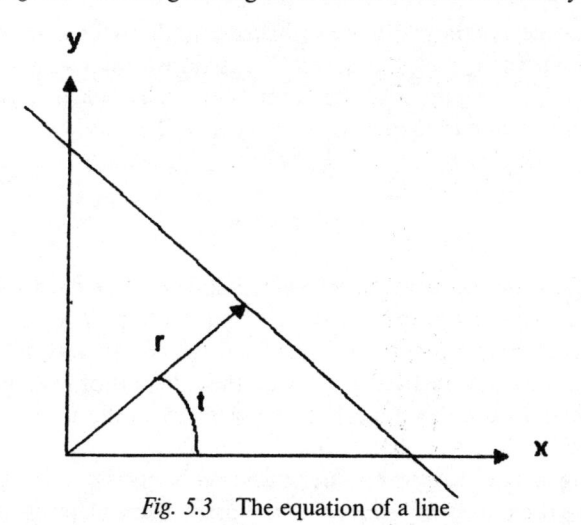

Fig. 5.3 The equation of a line

$$x_i\cos t + y_i\sin t = r$$

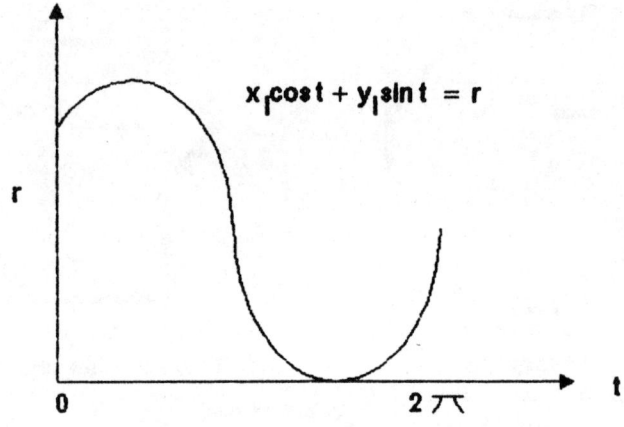

Fig. 5.4 The Hough transform of a point x_i y_j

If a number of points lie on the same line, i.e. are collinear, then their Hough transforms intersect in a single point in r t space. Thus to detect edge or line segments which lie on the same line all we have to do is to compute the Hough transform of each point and count the number of intersections in Hough space. Notice that this procedure doesn't take any account of the direction indicated by the edge or line segment. To do this would require restrictions to be placed on the values of r and t in Hough space. The Hough transform can be generalised to detect groups of points lying on any sort of curve. If the curve is given by a function such as:

$$f(a_1, a_2, \ldots a_n, x, y) = 0$$

where $a_1, a_2, \ldots a_n$ are the parameters which define the exact form of the curve, then for each point x_i y_i its generalised Hough transform is a surface given by $f(a_1, a_2, \ldots a_n)$. The complexity of the Hough transform increases very rapidly with the number of parameters needed to define the curve.

Relaxation

Relaxation is an iterative method of segmentation designed to assign pixels to regions based on some property, taking into account the assignment of their neighbours. It is an iterative process because of the way in which the assignment of each pixel has to affect all the others. For example, initially pixels are identified as being part of line segments without reference to the classification of their neighbours, but there is clearly an increased chance of a pixel being in a line segment if one of its neighbours is already identified as such. Relaxation starts off with an initial assignment of pixels to different types of region and then re-evaluates the assignment of each pixel to see how compatible it is with the assignment of its neighbours. If the initial assignment is incompatible, it is changed to make it more compatible. After every pixel in the image has been examined, the whole process is repeated until nothing changes, i.e. the assignment has relaxed into its final form.

There are many different versions of the relaxation method depending on what types of region are being considered and on the meaning given to 'compatibility'. One particularly general formulation is based on the probability of a pixel belonging to a particular region or class. The initial assignment corresponds to giving each pixel a_i (for simplicity only one index will be used to denote pixel location) a probability p_{ih}^0 of belonging to class h. The compatibility of the assignment of pixel i and pixel j is given by c(i,h:j,k) where pixel i is currently assigned to class h and pixel j is currently assigned to class k. Compatibility ranges from −1, strong incompatibility, through 0, neutral compatibilty, to +1, strong compatibility. Each iteration of the relaxation algorithm produces a new estimate of the probability p_{ih}^r where r is the number of iterations performed. There are three possibilities for the way that P_{ih}^r should be altered at each stage – if p_{ih}^r is high and c(i,h:j,k) tends to be is positive for its neighbours, p_{ih}^r should be increased; on the other hand if p_{ih}^r is high and c(i,h:j,k) tends to be is negative for its neighbours, p_{ih}^r should be decreased; finally if p_{ih}^r is low or if c(i,h:j,k) tends to be near 0 for its neighbours, p_{ih}^r should be left unchanged.

The rth iteration can be seen to involve the following stages:

For each pixel:

(1) Compute the average neighbour compatibility for pixel i being assigned to class h (for all values of h):

$$a(i,h) = \frac{1}{n} \sum_{\substack{k=1 \\ j=1(j \neq i)}} c(i,h:j,k) p_{jk}^r$$

(2) Update the probabilities p_{ih}^r using:

$$P_{ih}^{r+1} = \frac{p_{ih}^r(1+a(i,h))}{\sum_{h=1} p_{ih}^r(1+a(i,h))}$$

As this process is iterated, the probabilities tend to converge to either 1 or 0 so that each pixel may be associated to the class k for which $p_{ik}^r = 1$.

As an example of relaxation, consider its application to the simple threshold problem. In this case, there are only two classes, background or dark pixels and foreground or light pixels. Thus, for each point we have only two probabilities, p_{i1} and p_{i2} and $p_{i2}=1-p_{i1}$. The compatibilities can be chosen in a number of ways, but it seems reasonable that $c(i,1:j,1)=c(i,2:j,2)=c_{11}>0$ and $c(i,1:j,2)=c(i,2:j,1)=c_{12}<0$. The initial probabilities could also be assigned in a number of ways but a_i/a_{max} is a reasonable choice because it could be interpreted as a crude estimate of the probability that the pixel should be considered 'bright'. Thus, at the first iteration the increments are:

$$p_{i1}^1 = \sum_j \frac{1}{a_{max}} [c_{11}a_j + c_{12}(a_{max}-a_j)]$$

$$p_{i2}^1 = \sum_j \frac{1}{a_{max}} [c_{21}a_j + c_{22}(a_{max}-a_j)]$$

This can be thought of as a weighted average, but as it is iterated the probability of each point converges to 0 or 1, making final thresholding trivial. If you try this process you will discover that if most of the grey levels are on one side of the mean, the result will sometimes be an all black or all white image.

Texture

So far it has been assumed that homogeneous regions in an image tend to have the same average grey level which is different from other regions in the image – that is, segmentation is based on average tone. It is obvious that this is not always the case. Regions may have exactly the same average grey level but be visually quite different due to the way in which the grey levels are arranged to form a *texture*. Natural textures are common and familiar but their structure is surprisingly complex, and segmenting an image into regions consisting of homogeneous regions is quite difficult. A texture can roughly be said to be composed of a repetition of a basic unit. The repetition and the basic unit can be entirely regular or there can be an element of randomness in each or both (see Fig. 5.5). However, there are textures which show no obvious fixed basic unit nor fixed pattern of repetition.

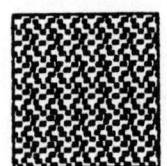

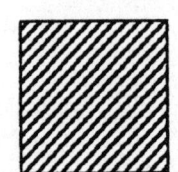

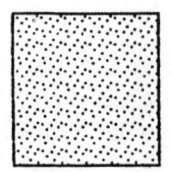

Fig. 5.5 Four sample textures showing regularity and irregularity

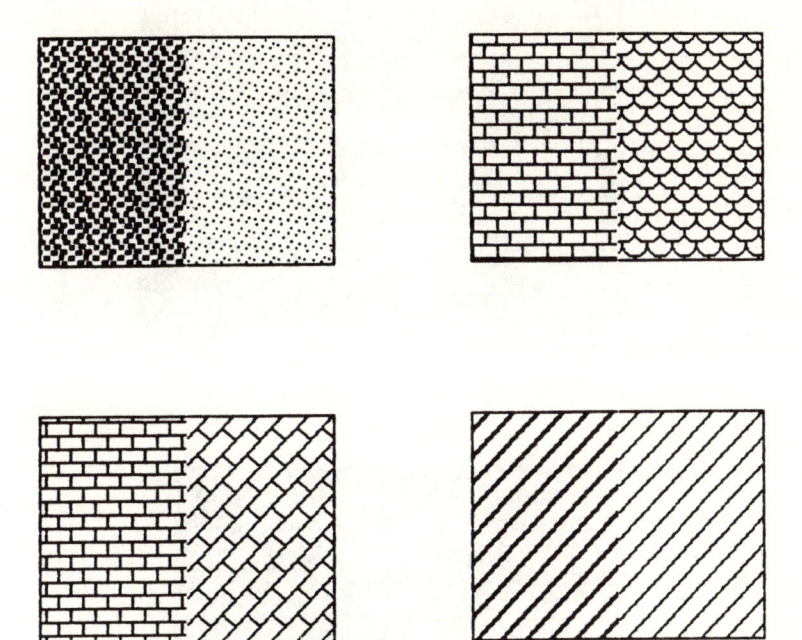

Fig. 5.6 Four sample texture edges

The presence of different textures in an image naturally results in the presence of, and hence the need to detect, *texture edges* (see Fig. 5.6).

There are two approaches to texture analysis – *statistical* and *structural*. The structural approach attempts to break the texture down into its basic units and repetition pattern. For example, you could use a local feature detector to find the position of various sizes of blobs in the texture, and then attempt to describe the repetition pattern revealed. Currently structural approaches are more difficult and not as well developed or understood as the statistical approach.

The statistical approach uses measures of the local grey level statistics. First order statistics are based on properties of single pixels, second order statistics describe how properties vary in pairs of pixels, third order statistics consider triplets and so on. (To be exact, nth order statistics depend on the joint probability distribution of n pixels.) For example, the grey level histogram is an example of a first order statistic in that it only depends on individual pixel grey levels. Second order statistics describe the way grey levels tend to occur together in pairs and in this way provide a measure of the type of texture present. This has an important psychological result in that the human visual system cannot distinguish textures which have the same first and second order statistics but different third order statistics. (There are a

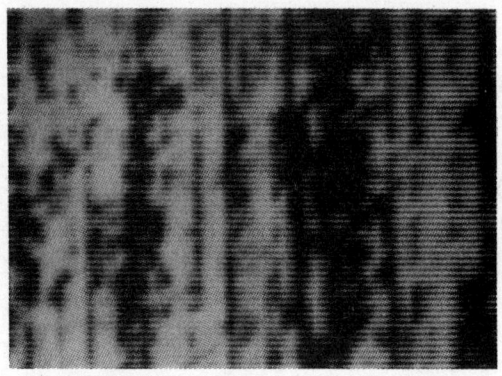

(a) Original image of wood bark

(b) Horizontal co-occurrence matrix

(c) Vertical co-occurrence matrix

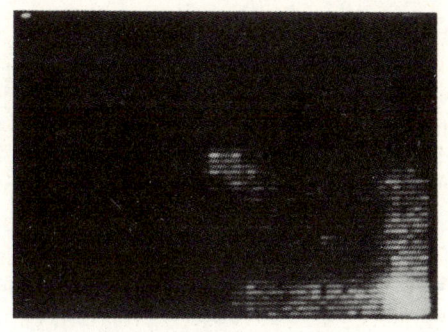

(d) Left diagonal co-occurrence matrix

(e) Right diagonal co-occurrence matrix

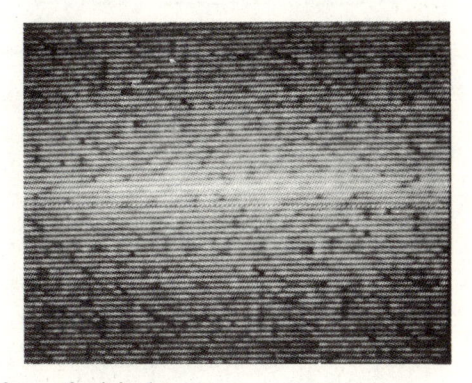

(f) Fourier transform of original

Plate 7 Texture analysis – 1

96 Pattern Recognition

number of counter examples to this rule but they all consist of discernable micro-patterns and the local second order statistics differ even if the global values are the same.) As only second order statistics seem to be used by the human visual system it makes sense to concentrate on these.

Co-occurrence matrices

The *co-occurrence matrix* is an estimate of the second order joint probability density. The joint probability distribution is P(i,j,d,t), the probability of grey levels i and j occurring at distance d and angle t. A co-occurrence matrix for distance d and angle t is composed of elements h_{ij} which record the number of pixel pairs d units apart in direction t, with one at grey level i and one at grey level j, the order being immaterial. Notice that a co-occurrence matrix is defined so as to be symmetric and that the estimation of the complete second order probability distribution requires co-occurrence matrices for all values of d and t. For example, given the image:

2	2	1	1
2	1	0	0
3	2	2	1
0	2	1	1

its co-occurrence matrix for d=1 and t=0 (i.e. horizontal pairs) is:

	0	1	2	3
0	2	1	1	0
1	1	4	4	0
2	1	4	4	1
3	0	0	1	0

It is assumed that all the information about the texture of an image is contained in its co-occurrence matrices but, rather than use all of the elements in a classification rule, a number of *texture measures* (or *textural features*) have been suggested which summarise some of the information that they contain. The following are three such measures.

$$f_1 = \sum_i \sum_j p(i,j)^2$$

is a measure of homogeneity of texture. For a uniform region the co-occurrence matrix contains a small number of large values and hence f_1 is large.

$$f_2 = \sum_{k=0}^{n-1} k^2 \sum_{|i-j|=k} p(i,j)$$

is a measure of the change in grey level in the texture, i.e. it is a measure of contrast.

$$f_3 = \frac{\sum_{ij} ijp(i,j) - \mu_x(i)\mu_y(j)}{\sigma_x(i)\sigma_y(j)}$$

where μ_x and μ_y are the row and column means and σ_x and σ_y are the row and column standard deviations, is a measure of correlation and it responds to highly ordered structures within textures. There are many other texture measures but these three are relatively simple to calculate and are successful at classifying different textures. In practice, it is not possible to construct very many co-occurrence matrices and, as long as the image scale is chosen accordingly, a value of d equal to one and values of t equal to 0°, 45°, 80° and 135° are often sufficient (i.e. only 4 matrices). However, the size of the co-occurrence matrix increases rapidly with the number of grey levels, as does the amount of work in constructing it.

A subroutine to calculate a co-occurrence matrix

The following subroutine will calculate any one of the 4 co-occurrence matrices corresponding to the directions; horizontal t%=1, vertical t%=2, diagonal 1 t%=3 and diagonal 2 t%=4 at a distance specified by d%. The input image is stored in im% and the resulting co-occurrence matrix is returned in pr% both two-dimensional with im% nn% by nn% and the size of pr% set large enough to deal with the number of grey levels in use. Notice how when a pair of pixels with grey levels a% and b% have been found both pr%(a%,b%) and pr%(b%,a%) are incremented to keep the matrix symmetric.

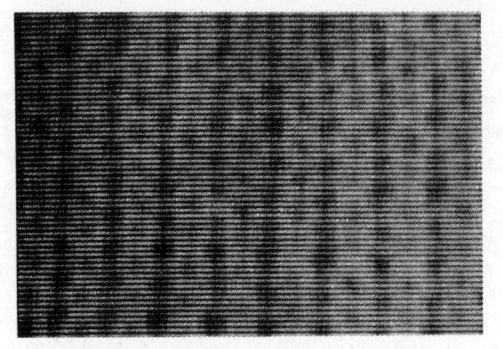

(a) Original image of knitted wool

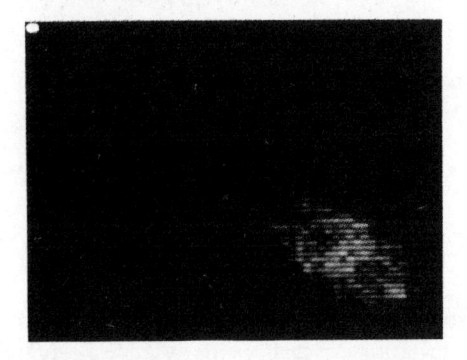

(b) Horizontal co-occurrence matrix

(c) Vertical co-occurrence matrix

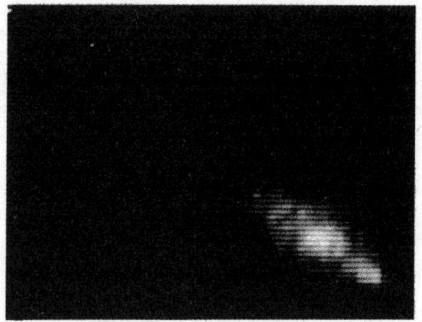

(d) Left diagonal co-occurrence matrix

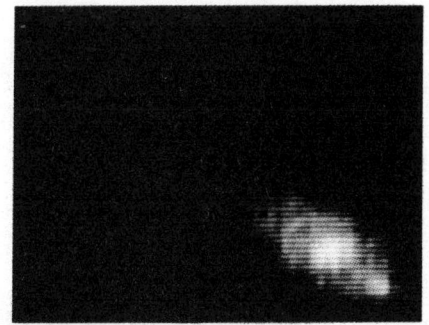

(e) Right diagonal co-occurrence matrix

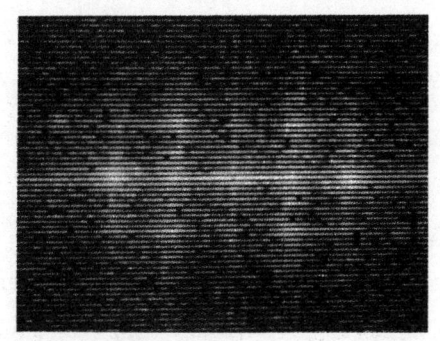

(f) Fourier transform of original

Plate 8 Texture analysis – 2

```
SUB cooc(im%(2),pr%(2),nn%,t%,d%) STATIC
  REM set up boundaries of scan
   for different directions
  si%=0
  IF t%=1 THEN id%=d%:jd%=0
  IF t%=2 THEN id%=0:jd%=d%
  IF t%=3 THEN id%=d%:jd%=d%
  IF t%=4 THEN id%=-d%:jd%=d%:si%=d%
  REM scan array counting pairs
  FOR i%=si% TO nn%-ABS(id%)-si%
   FOR j%=0 TO nn%-jd%
    a%=im%(i%,j%)
    b%=im%(i%+id%,j%+jd%)
    REM the grey level at i%,j% is a%
        and at i%+id%,j%+jd% is b%
    REM increment the appropriate co-occurrence
        matrix elements
    pr%(a%,b%)=pr%(a%,b%)+1
    pr%(b%,a%)=pr%(b%,a%)+1
   NEXT j%
  NEXT i%
END SUB
```

Local Feature Statistics

Although co-occurrence matrices seem to get to the theoretical heart of texture structure and analysis, they do not provide a practical solution for most problems. One practical but *ad hoc* solution is to use statistics relating to the distribution of local features. For example, a simple gradient operator can be used to determine the 'busyness' of an image by measuring the number of edges per unit area. This can be used to extract regions of similar texture by:

(1) Applying the difference operator to the image.
(2) Working out the average within a given local region across the entire image i.e.applying an averaging operator.
(3) Tresholding the image to separate busy areas from quiet ones.

The averaging operation gives an image with values proportional to the number of edges in the local region. This method can be extended to other local operators, used for example, to detect the local density of lines or blobs. An alternative approach is to work out statistics other than the mean such as the standard deviation within the local area. At a more sophisticated level, you could even consider constructing co-occurrence matrices and their associated measures on images which result from the application of local feature detectors.

Fourier texture features

As textures tend to contain periodic or semi-periodic components, an obvious approach to texture analysis is to use the components of the Fourier transform as texture measures. Typical texture measures consist of filters in the form of anular rings and strips of different orientation in the spectrum. The disadvantage of the Fourier method is that textures tend to be random and their aperiodic nature often results in a confused spectrum. The exception to this is, of course, in the case of a completely regular texture, like the bricks in a brick wall. Such regular textures tend to be man-made and, as such, Fourier texture features are often said to be good at separating natural and artificial textures. In practice, textural features based on second order statistics or on the distribution of local features seem to perform better and they are generally easier to calculate.

Chapter Six
Binary Images

The most practical area of image processing at present is concerned with the processing of binary images, i.e. two-valued images. If you can obtain a suitable binary image showing the required object, then there are a wide range of techniques which you can use to enhance the image and extract features that make classification possible. Binary image processing is easier from both the theoretical and practical point of view. Binary images are more amenable to analysis because they have clear cut properties such as boundaries, areas and shape. Because only two values, usually 0 and 1, are needed to represent brightness levels, they can be processed using *Boolean* operators (e.g. AND, OR and NOT) which are faster than integer or floating point arithmetic.

Although binary image processing is a field in which much can be achieved, it is important not to lose sight of one of its fundamental problems – obtaining the binary image. Nearly all binary image processing starts off from the premise 'given a binary image with the following properties' and then shows how enhancement, analysis or recognition can be achieved. Of course, this begs the practical question of how such a binary image can be obtained, and as other chapters have suggested, this can be 99% of the real image processing/recognition problem!

Boolean operations on binary images

A binary image can be represented by an array of zeros and ones and as such can be manipulated by the use of *Boolean* or *logical* operators rather than by arithmetic. If you add or subtract two binary images or perform local operations analagous to convolution on a binary image the result is not a binary image but a multi-valued grey level image. The advantage of binary processing from the point of view of storage and simplicity of interpretation is that it can aim to produce one binary image from another. The Boolean operators AND, OR, XOR (exclusive or) and NOT are suitable for mapping one binary image into another and producing useful results. The effect of the four operations can be seen from the following truth tables:

AND

A	B	A AND B
0	0	0
0	1	0
1	0	0
1	1	1

OR

A	B	A OR B
0	0	0
0	1	1
1	0	1
1	1	1

EOR

A	B	A EOR B
0	0	0
0	1	1
1	0	1
1	1	0

NOT

A	NOT A
0	1
1	0

The effect of applying each of these operations pointwise to a pair of Boolean images is shown in Figure 6.1.

Properties of binary images

As a binary image is composed unequivocally of foreground and background pixels, many of the classical geometric and topological properties can be applied. For example, we can ask questions about the shape of a *binary object* because it has well-defined boundaries. Questions about the shape of an object in a grey level image depend on where we decide its edges are. Notice that while the shape of a binary object is well defined, this shape may not correspond to the shape of any object in a grey level image or in the real world from which the binary image was derived and is supposed to represent. For example, a grey level image of an unevenly illuminated sphere may appear to have a disk-like shape, but a binary image obtained by simple thresholding, while having a definite shape, is certain to be anything but disk-shaped.

Most binary processing concentrates on obtaining measures of the shape etc. of the image as presented without being concerned with how this relates to reality or to the original grey level image. Of course, in a complete image processing/recognition system such questions would be vitally important.

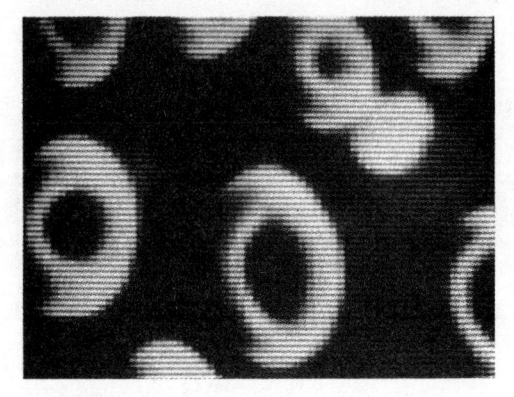

(a) Original image of blood cells

(b) Binary image derived from original

(c) Four-connected boundary

(d) Eight-connected boundary – notice the 'missing' points in right angled corners

Plate 9 Boundary finding

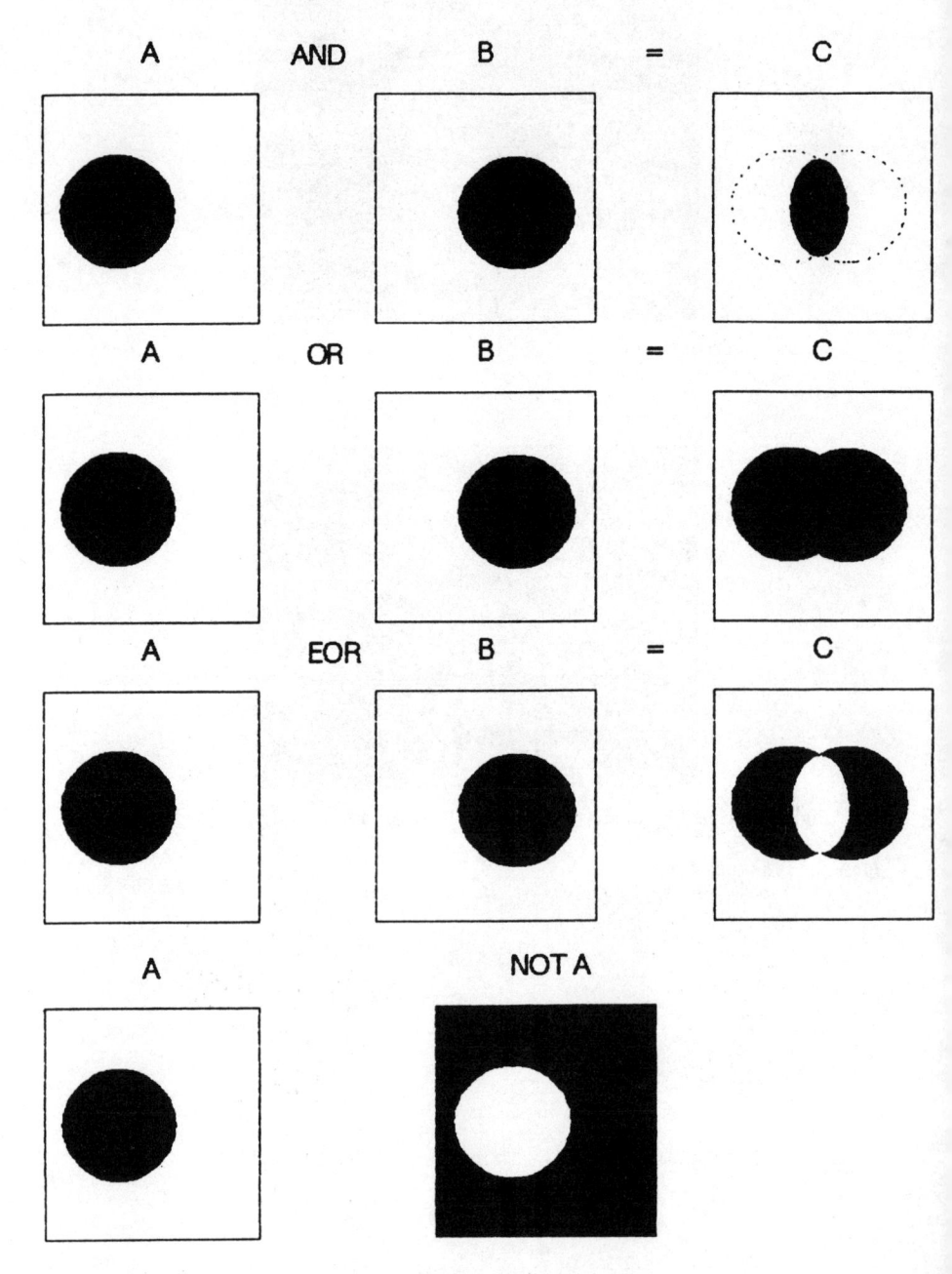

Fig. 6.1 Boolean operations

Grey level image   Binary image

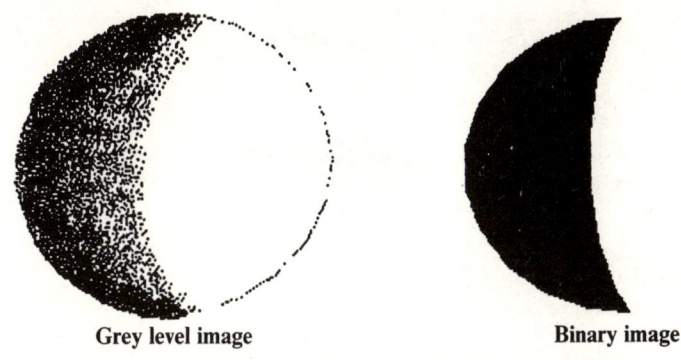

Fig. 6.2 The difficulty in selecting a threshold

Binary edges: 4- and 8-connectivity

Given a binary object, it is possible to distinguish two types of pixel – interior pixels which have no immediate neighbours that are part of the background, and border pixels which do have at least one immediate neighbour that is part of the background. The set of border pixels form a *boundary* or *binary edge* for the object. The sort of boundary obtained depends on the definition used for a pixel's immediate neighbours. The key idea is that of *connectedness*. A border pixel is connected to the background whereas an interior pixel is not. There are two definitions of connectivity – *8-connected* and *4-connected*. A pixel can be defined as being connected to either its eight nearest neighbours i.e. 8-connected, or to its four horizontal and vertical neighbours i.e. 4-connected (see Fig. 6.3).

8-connected   **4-connected**

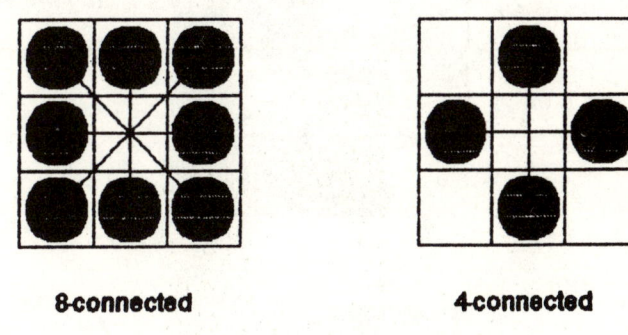

Fig. 6.3 4- and 8-connectivity

The 8-connected definition makes sense because the central pixel actually touches the four diagonal pixels at each corner and hence in this way is indeed connected to them. The 4-connected definition also makes sense because the

108 *Pattern Recognition*

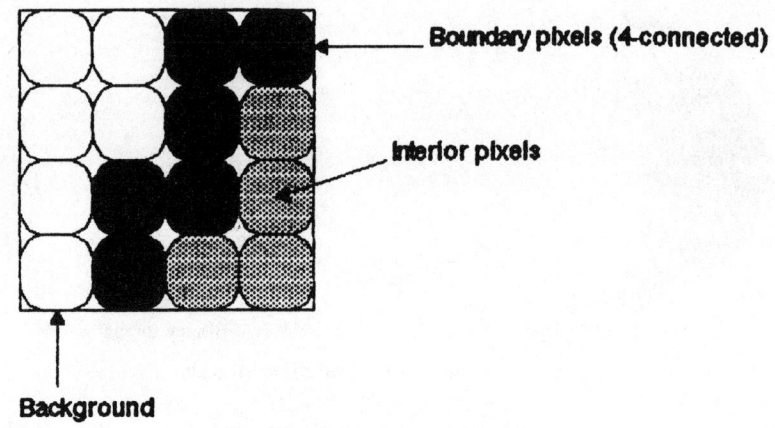

Fig. 6.4 A 4-connected boundary

four diagonal pixels are further away from the central pixel than the four non-diagonal neighbours.

There is a hidden paradox in both these definitions of connectivity. Suppose we take 8-connectedness as our definition of connectivity, then an object boundary consists of object pixels which are connected to the background and this produces a boundary that is itself 4-connected (see Fig. 6.4).

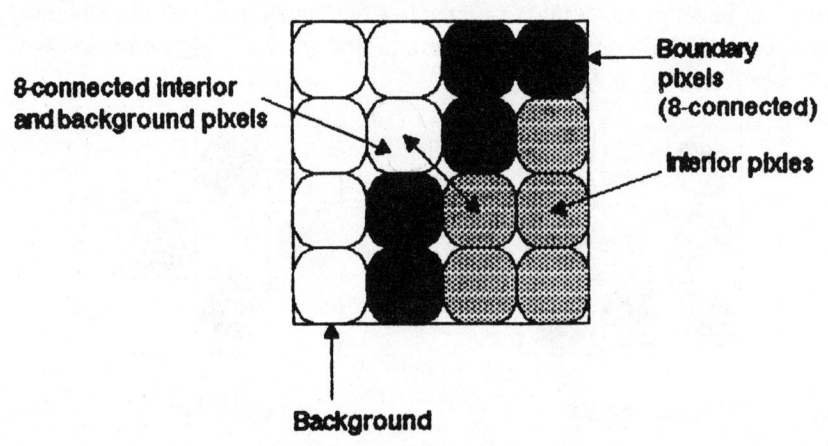

Fig. 6.5 An 8-connected boundary

If we attempt to reduce this boundary to a set of 8-connected pixels, we arrive at the paradoxical result that a connected closed boundary does not separate the interior pixels from the background. The reason for this is that if the boundary were reduced to just the 8-connected pixels necessary to make it connected, then some interior pixels, which were not part of the boundary, would also be connected to the background (see Fig. 6.5).

The same sort of problem results if we use the 4-connected definition. In this case the resulting boundary is not 4-connected but 8-connected and we have the strange result that while the points inside the boundary do not touch the points outside the boundary (in the 4-connected sense), the boundary points are themselves not connected.

The solution to this problem is to adopt different definitions of connectedness for the object (i.e. pixels with the value 1) and the background (i.e. pixels with the value 0). If the object pixels are considered 8-connected then the background should be considered 4-connected and vice versa. A practical example of this is to be found in the description of boundary extraction operators.

Local Boolean operators

In the same way that masking operations or convolution are the basic operations for grey level images, *local Boolean* operations are the starting point for all binary image processing. A local Boolean operation is like a convolution in the sense that it can be thought of as combining a mask with the image at every possible position in the image but, instead of arithmetic, Boolean logic is used. Each element of the mask is ANDed with the corresponding element of the image and the results are further combined to produce a single result using NOT and OR. (As in the case of convolution the results of the operation are stored in a new array and the original image is not altered in any way.) To avoid unnecessary shifts, the result of the masking operation is stored in the pixel defined by the centre of the mask.

Although this is an interesting way to think of local Boolean operators, it is more useful to regard them as general Boolean functions involving a pixel and its nearest neighbours. That is, a local Boolean operator is:

$$a_{ij} = F(a_{ij}, \text{ and its neighbours})$$

where F is a Boolean function made up of any Boolean operators such as AND, OR, NOT or EOR. It is simpler to specify a Boolean operation in this way if we just consider a 3 × 3 arrangement of pixels numbered as:

Pattern Recognition

a_1	a_2	a_3
a_8	a_0	a_4
a_7	a_6	a_5

and state the Boolean function in terms of just these pixels but remembering to repeat the operation at all positions within the image.

A Boolean operator for boundary points

A boundary point is a foreground pixel that has at least one neighbour that is a background pixel. The condition for at least one 8-connected neighbour being a background pixel can be written:

$$B = (\text{NOT } a_1) \text{ OR } (\text{NOT } a_2) \text{ OR } (\text{NOT } a_3)$$
$$\text{OR } (\text{NOT } a_4) \text{ OR } (\text{NOT } a_5) \text{ OR } (\text{NOT } a_6)$$
$$\text{OR } (\text{NOT } a_7) \text{ OR } (\text{NOT } a_8)$$

which is 1 if any of a_1 to a_8 is 0. All that has to be added to this Boolean function to give us our boundary point detector is an extra condition that only if B is 1 and a_0 is 1 is the final result 1. In other words, our final local Boolean operator is:

$$a_0 \text{ AND } B$$

which, of course, has to be applied to every pixel in the image. Most local operators divide into these two parts, one which detects a certain configuration of a_1 to a_8 and another which combines this with the original value of the image a_0. As the neighbours of a_0 were considered to be 8-connected, the resulting border pixels will be 4-connected. This is usually referred to as P_4 or the *4-connected perimeter* operator. The equivalent *8-connected perimeter* operator P_8 is obtained by replacing B by (NOT a_2) OR (NOT a_4) OR (NOT a_6) OR (NOT a_8).

A subroutine to find boundary points

The following subroutine will find all the boundary in the image array bi% storing the results in obi%, both nn% by nn%. If s%=4, a 4-connected boundary is produced. If s%=8, an 8-connected boundary is produced. The images must be stored using BASIC's true value for foreground pixels and its false value for background pixels. (For Quick BASIC and most Microsoft BASICs true is –1 and false is 0.)

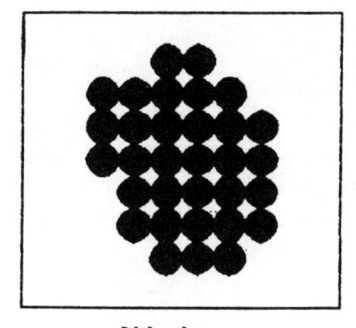

Object

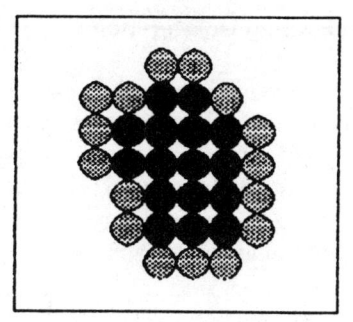

8-connected boundary

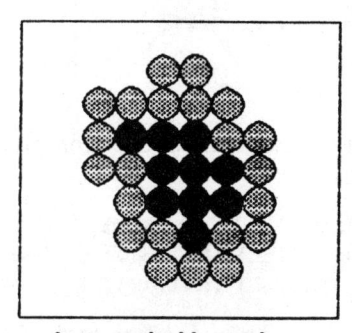

4-connected boundary

Fig. 6.6 Finding boundary points

```
SUB bound(bi%(2),obi%(2),nn%,s%) STATIC
  FOR x%=1 TO nn%-2
   FOR y%=1 TO nn%-2
    REM compute b
    bh%=(NOT bi%(x%-1,y%)) OR (NOT bi%(x%+1,y%))
    bh%=bh% OR (NOT bi%(x%,y%-1))
         OR (NOT bi%(x%,y%+1))
    bd%=(NOT bi%(x%-1,y%-1))
         OR (NOT bi%(x%-1,y%+1))
    bd%=bd% OR (NOT bi%(x%+1,y%-1))
         OR (NOT bi%(x%+1,y%+1))
    REM 4 or 8 boundary
    IF s%=8 THEN b%=bh% ELSE b%=bh% OR bd%
    REM find boundary points
     obi%(x%,y%)=b% AND bi%(x%,y%)
   NEXT y%
  NEXT x%
END SUB
```

112 Pattern Recognition

Finding isolated points

Isolated points within a binary image are most probably caused by noise, so a good first operation to apply to any image is one that would remove such points. It is very easy to formulate a local Boolean operator that does just that. An isolated point is a foreground (i.e. value 1) pixel that has no foreground pixels as its neighbours. That is, we are trying to detect and eliminate any 3 × 3 local area that looks like:

A local Boolean function that would give a 1 for this pattern of neighbours and a 0 for all others is simply:

$$B = (NOT\ a_1)\ AND\ (NOT\ a_2)\ AND\ (NOT\ a_3)$$
$$AND\ (NOT\ a_4)\ AND\ (NOT\ a_5)\ AND\ (NOT\ a_6)$$
$$AND\ (NOT\ a_7)\ AND\ (NOT\ a_8)$$

In other words, all eight neighbours have to be 0 to make B equal to 1. To remove isolated noise points any pixel a_0 that is a 1 and for which B is also a 1 should result in a 0 and all other pixels should produce a result equal to their original value. Thus the local Boolean operator is:

$$a_0\ AND\ NOT\ B$$

A subroutine to remove noise points

The following subroutine removes noise points from the image stored in bi%, placing the result in obi% both nn% by nn%. Once again the images must be stored using true for foreground pixels and false for background pixels – see the boundary detection subroutine given on page 111.

```
SUB rnoise(bi%(2),obi%(2),nn%) STATIC
FOR x%=1 TO nn%-2
 FOR y%=1 TO nn%-2
  REM calculate B
  b%=(NOT bi%(x%-1,y%)) AND (NOT bi%(x%+1,y%))
  b%=b% AND (NOT bi%(x%,y%-1))
      AND (NOT bi%(x%,y%+1))
  b%=b% AND (NOT bi%(x%-1,y%-1))
```

```
        AND (NOT bi%(x%-1,y%+1))
   b%=b% AND (NOT bi%(x%+1,y%-1))
        AND (NOT bi%(x%+1,y%+1))
   REM calculate final result
   obi%(x%,y%)=(NOT b%) AND bi%(x%,y%)
  NEXT y%
 NEXT x%
END SUB
```

Shrink and expand – binary filtering

Shrink and expand are two very useful local Boolean operations that are in some ways analogous to grey level filtering. *Shrinking* a binary object makes it smaller by removing the pixels which constitute its boundary. That is, every pixel with at least one background neighbour is set to 0. The local Boolean operator is given by:

$$B = (NOT\ a_1)\ OR\ (NOT\ a_2)\ OR\ (NOT\ a_3)$$
$$OR\ (NOT\ a_4)\ OR\ (NOT\ a_5)\ OR\ (NOT\ a_6)$$
$$OR\ (NOT\ a_7)\ OR\ (NOT\ a_8)$$

$$Shrink\ =\ a_0\ AND\ NOT\ B$$

(This is an 8-connected definition of a shrink. The 4-connected version is obtained by ignoring the diagonal neighbours.) The repeated application of the shrink operation has an action that can best be imagined as stripping off the layers of an onion. Thus, loosely speaking, n shrinks will remove objects or parts of objects which can be said to be of size n.

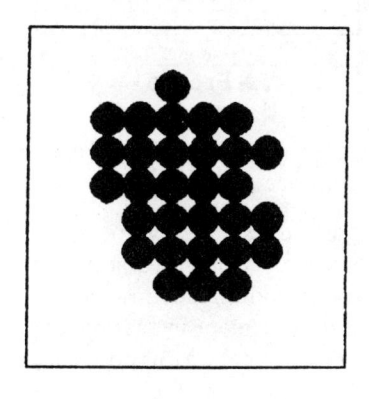

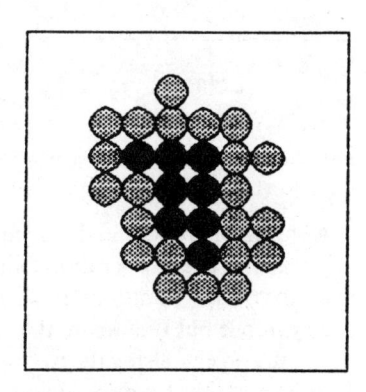

Fig. 6.7 A single shrink

114 Pattern Recognition

The *expand* operator is the reverse process to a shrink in that it adds to an object the background pixels which are next to a pixel in the object. You can think of this as adding a sort of outer boundary to the object. The local Boolean operator for the expand operation is:

$$B = (a_1) \text{ OR } (a_2) \text{ OR } (a_3)$$
$$\text{OR } (a_4) \text{ OR } (a_5) \text{ OR } (a_6)$$
$$\text{OR } (a_7) \text{ OR } (a_8)$$
$$\text{Expand} = \text{NOT } a_0 \text{ AND } B \text{ OR } a_0$$

(This is an 8-connected definition of an expand; a 4-connected definition can be obtained by ignoring the diagonal neighbours.)

In the same way that the shrink operation removes layers from an object, the expand operator adds them (see Fig. 6.8). The expand operator can be thought of as shrinking the background and, as you might guess from this, any holes in an object will eventually disappear.

Object

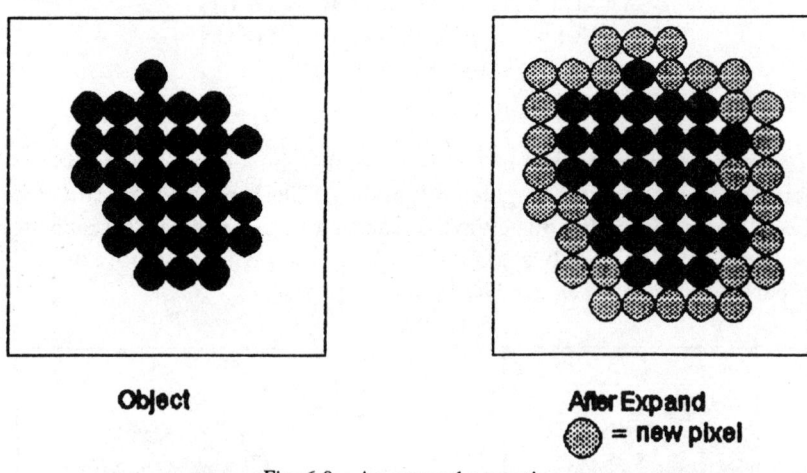

After Expand
◉ = new pixel

Fig. 6.8 An expand operation

A shrink operation tends to remove small objects and small projections on objects. An expand operation tends to fill holes and concavities in objects. In this sense, the operations have complementary smoothing actions on the binary image but they share the defect of either decreasing or increasing the size of the object. Using the two operations together overcomes this problem. That is, a shrink followed by an expand tends to remove small objects and projections without changing the overall size of an object, and an expand followed by a shrink tends to fill holes and concavities also without changing the overall size of the object.

Binary Images **115**

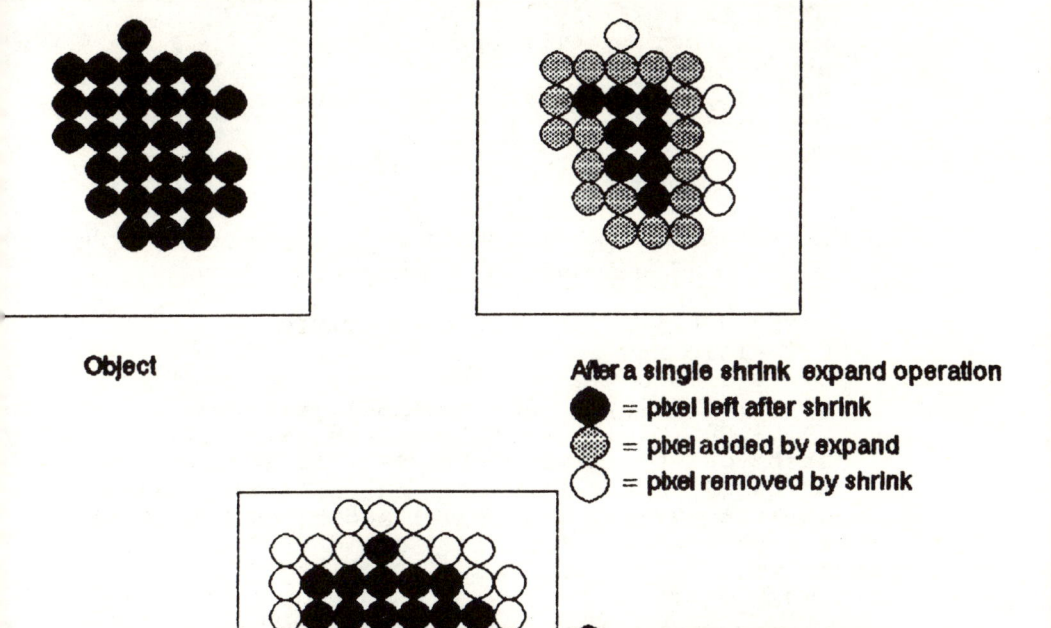

Fig. 6.9 Expand and shrink operation

hrink expand subroutines
he following subroutine will perform an 8-connected shrink on the image
ored in bi%, storing the result in obi%, both nn% by nn%. The images must
e stored so that foreground pixels are true and background pixels false – see
arlier subroutines in this chapter.

```
SUB shrink(bi%(2),obi%(2),nn%) STATIC
FOR x%=1 TO nn%-2
 FOR y%=1 TO nn%-2
  REM calculate B
  b%=(NOT bi%(x%-1,y%)) OR (NOT bi%(x%+1,y%))
  b%=b% OR (NOT bi%(x%,y%-1))
      OR (NOT bi%(x%,y%+1))
  b%=b% OR (NOT bi%(x%-1,y%-1))
```

```
        OR (NOT bi%(x%-1,y%+1))
  b%=b% OR (NOT bi%(x%+1,y%-1))
        OR (NOT bi%(x%+1,y%+1))
  REM final result
  obi%(x%,y%)=bi%(x%,y%) AND NOT b%
  NEXT y%
 NEXT x%
END SUB
```

The following subroutine will perform an 8-connected expand on the image stored in bi%, storing the result in obi%, both nn% by nn%.

```
SUB expand(bi%(2),obi%(2),nn%) STATIC
 FOR x%=1 TO nn%-2
  FOR y%=1 TO nn%-2
   b%=(bi%(x%-1,y%)) OR (bi%(x%+1,y%))
   b%=b% OR (bi%(x%,y%-1)) OR (bi%(x%,y%+1))
   b%=b% OR (bi%(x%-1,y%-1)) OR (bi%(x%-1,y%+1))
   b%=b% OR (bi%(x%+1,y%-1)) OR (bi%(x%+1,y%+1))
   obi%(x%,y%)=NOT bi%(x%,y%) AND b% OR bi%(x%,y%)
  NEXT y%
 NEXT x%
END SUB
```

Shape - area, perimeter and moments

If you have an image consisting of one binary object, the simplest measurements that you can take are its area and perimeter. Its area can be taken by simply counting the number of foreground pixels in the image. How this relates to the area of the real object before digitisation depends on how the digitisation was performed and magnification used. Measuring the perimeter can be achieved by counting the pixels in the boundary of the object, although this ignores a number of difficulties – in particular, that the distance between horizontal and vertical pixels is 1 but the distance between diagonal pixels is roughly 15% larger (see Fig. 6.10).

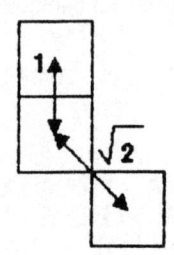

Fig. 6.10 The distances between pixels

An improved estimate of the perimeter can be achieved by counting the number of pixels in the P_8 and P_4 perimeters. The product P_8P_4 is a good approximation to P^2, the perimeter squared.

Classification of binary objects is mostly a matter of shape discrimination and so the type of features which we are looking for are *indices of shape* that are easy and quick to calculate. The best-known shape index is the *generalised pi* index. This is simply P^2/A, that is, the perimeter squared divided by the area of an object. This quantity is independent of changes in scale and rotation and is easy to compute although it doesn't have very good shape discrimination power. It can, however, discriminate between classes of simple regular geometric shapes such as squares, triangles and ellipses.

For general shapes there is a theoretical solution based on *moments*. The (i,j) moment of an object is defined as:

$$m_{ij} = \sum_{xy} x^i y^j a_{xy}$$

which, because in a binary image a_{xy} is either 1 or 0, reduces to a sum of $x^i y^j$ for all the pixels in the object. The complete set of moments provides an exact description of the shape of an object but each moment is not invariant to shifts or change of scale. Moments can be made invariant to shifts by calculating *central moments*. The *centroid* of an object is:

$$\bar{x} = \frac{m_{10}}{m_{00}} \qquad \bar{y} = \frac{m_{01}}{m_{00}}$$

and the (i,j) central moment is:

$$\bar{m}_{ij} = \sum_{xy} (x-\bar{x})^i (y-\bar{y})^j$$

To produce shape indices from central moments which are invariant to changes in scale, all that is necessary is to use ratios of moments that have the same value of i+j, e.g. m_{23}/m_{32}. Some central moments are well known by other names – m_{00} is the area of the object and m_{02} and m_{20} are the moments of intertia.

Binary mask matching

Moments can be used to classify objects based on shape but calculating them is very time-consuming. One alternative is to use convolution with suitably shaped binary masks. Each mask would be designed to detect either a whole target shape such as a spanner, or standard sub-shapes such as squares and

118 *Pattern Recognition*

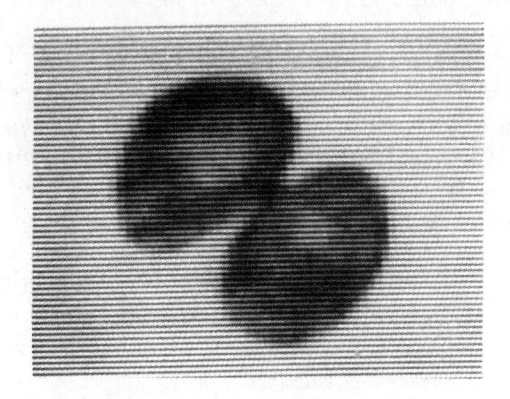

(a) Original image of two cells

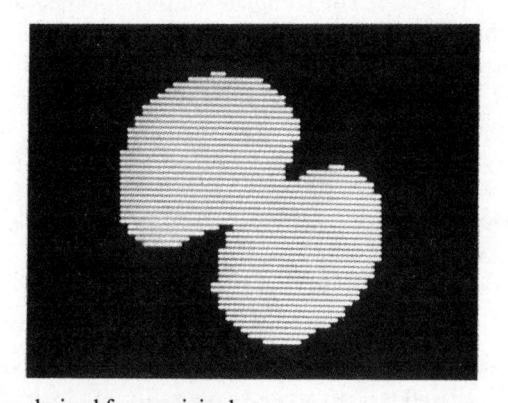

(b) Binary image derived from original

Plate 10 Using shrink/expand to separate objects

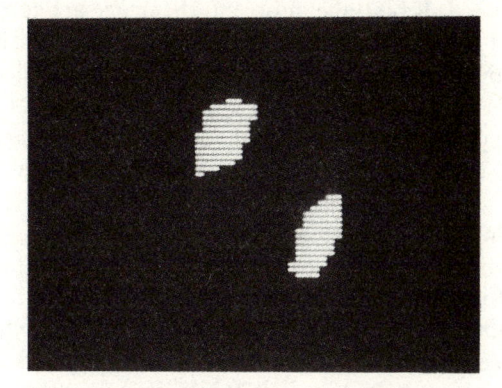

(c) Result of repeated shrinking

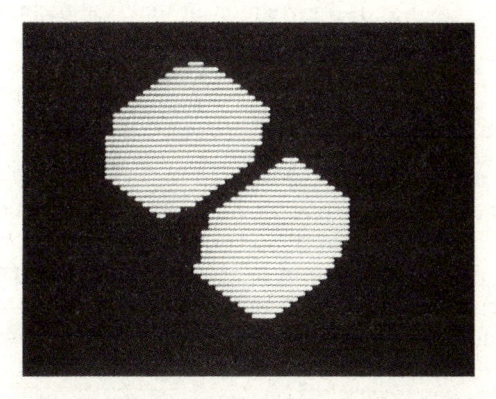

(d) Result of repeated expanding

120 Pattern Recognition

circles. Some care has to be taken about how a convolution with a binary mask is calculated. If both the mask and the image are composed of pixels with binary 0 1 values, the simple convolution is equal to the number of times a pixel with value 1 in the mask is matched by a pixel with value 1 in the image. In other words, simple convolution only takes into account matches between ones in the mask and the image. Thus the convolution reaches a maximum on an area of the image composed of all ones, no matter what shape the mask has!

The solution is to use a normalised measure of how well the mask matches the image. This can be obtained by dividing the result of the convolution at each point in the image by the number of ones in the area of the image covered by the convolution mask. Another alternative is to change the mask so that matches between zeros are as important as matches between ones. This can be done by replacing every 0 in the mask by –1 and using this as a convolution mask. Now positions in the mask that were 0 contribute negatively to the result of the convolution if they correspond to ones in the image. Thus using a mask made up of 1 and –1 gives a result that is a maximum for a perfect match.

Boundaries and shape

One possible approach to the measurement of shape concentrates on the description of an object's boundary curve. An object's outline as defined by its boundary is a complete description of the object in the sense that the object can easily be reconstructed from it. However, the number of pixels in the boundary is considerably smaller than the number in the whole object and hence it should be more efficient to calculate shape indices from it. Most boundary methods start by reducing the two-dimensional representation of the boundary to a one-dimensional representation by the use of a *chain code*. If each neighbour of the pixel a_0 is labelled as shown below:

0	1	2
7	a_0	3
6	5	4

then a boundary, or any other curve, can be specified by starting from an arbitrary point and repeatedly giving the number of the next pixel in the chain. For example, the chain code of the curve:

Binary Images 121

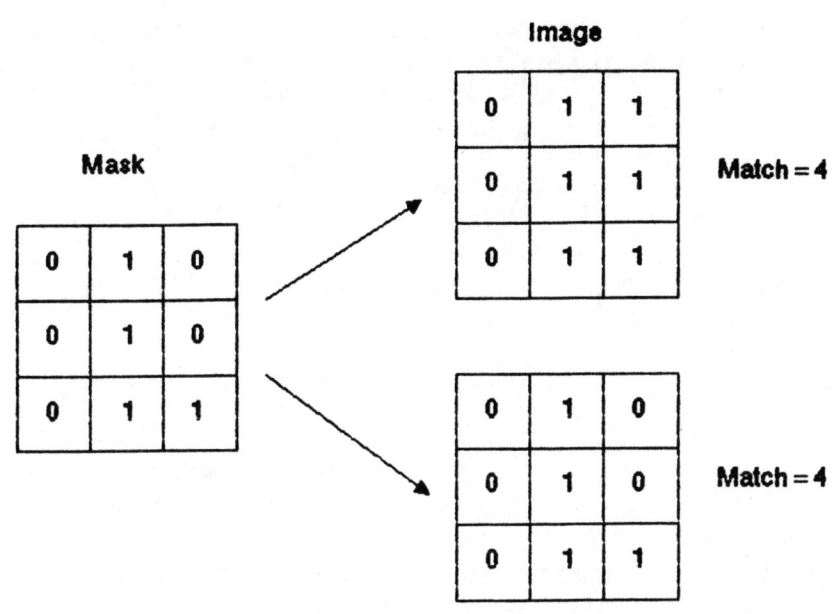

Fig. 6.11 Binary mask matching

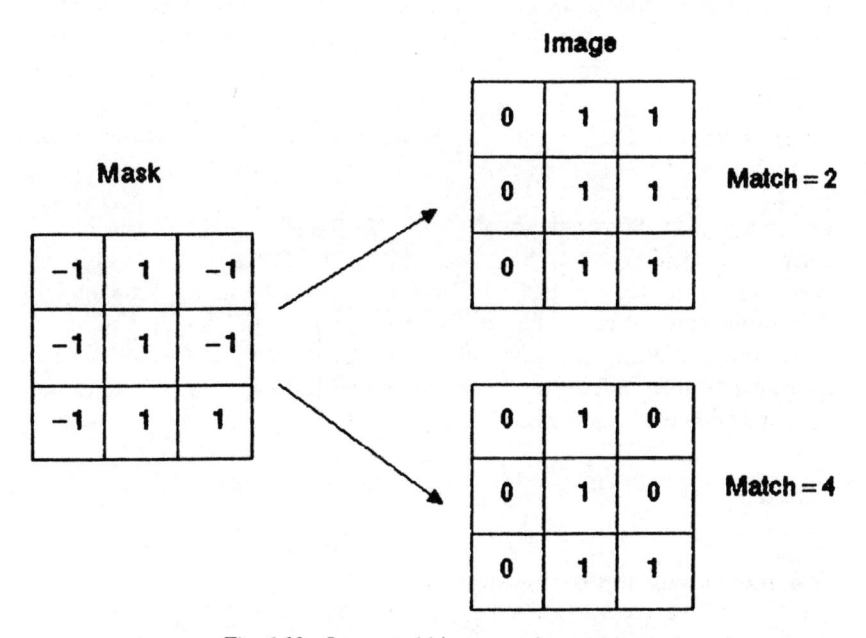

Fig. 6.12 Improved binary mask matching

122 Pattern Recognition

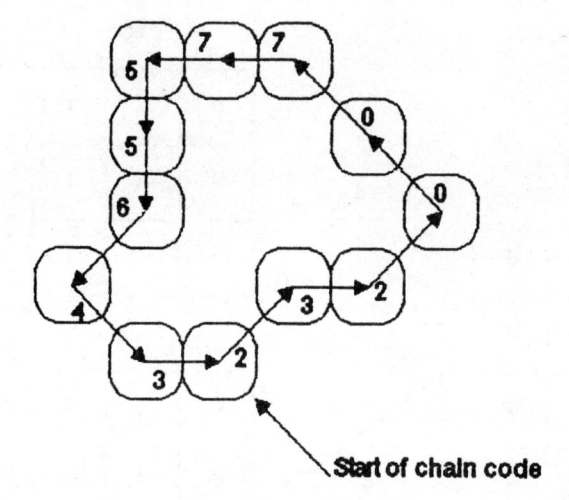

Start of chain code

is 232007755643. Notice that as a chain code can obviously be used to reconstruct the curve from which it was derived (apart from its absolute position which could be supplied by giving the co-ordinates of the first point of curve) and the object can be reconstructed from its outline, the chain code of a boundary is sufficient to reconstruct the object. Thus a chain code provides a very efficient way of storing the description of a binary object.

The similarity of two curves or boundaries x and y can be measured by computing:

$$S_{xy} = \frac{1}{n}\sum_{i=1}^{n} x_i . y_i$$

(where $x_i . y_i$ is COS[angle(x_i)–angle(y_i)]). This can be thought of as a sort of correlation coefficient for chain encoded curves. This is only useful if the curves are of the same scale, length and coded from the same starting point. The problem of the possible different starting point can be solved by computing a chain code equivalent of convolution, that is working out the measure of similarity for one of the chain codes shifted against the second and then choosing the largest value:

$$S_{xy}(k) = \frac{1}{m}\sum_{i=1}^{m} x_i . y_{i+k}$$

The medial axis and skeletonisation

The use of boundaries to describe the shape of an object has a parallel in the

Binary Images **123**

use of *internal cores* or *skeletons* of objects. The best example of skeleton is the way a stick man figure is used to represent the shape of the human body. For many purposes a skeleton is an adequate description of the shape of an object.

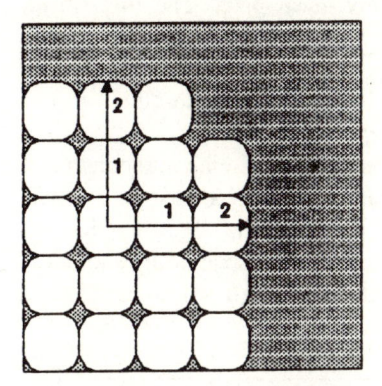

Two shortest 4-connected paths
The 4 depth of the pixel is 2

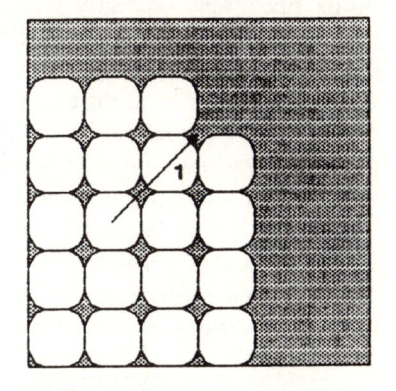

A shortest 8-connected path
The 8 depth of the pixel is 1

Fig. 6.13   The depth of a pixel

One definition of a skeleton of an object is the set of points which are in the middle of the shape. This idea corresponds to the *medial axis transformation* or MAT of the shape. To define the MAT we first have to say what is meant by the distance of a point within an object from the background. There are many possible definitions for digital distance but the most natural is to define the distance of a point from the background as the length of the shortest 4- or

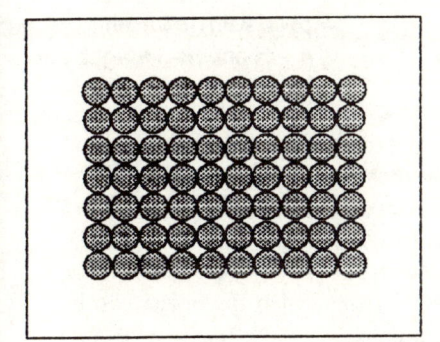

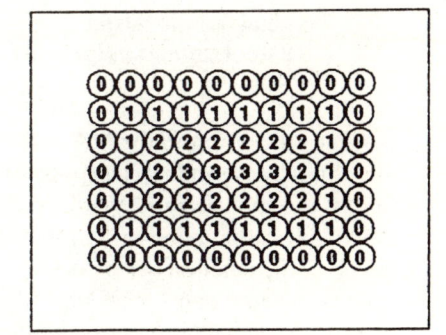

An object and its depth map
(Notice that the map is the same for 4 and 8-distance)

Fig. 6.14   The depth map

124 Pattern Recognition

8-connected path within the object to a background pixel. The length of the path is most simply interpreted to mean the number of pixels in the path.

This definition of distance also corresponds to one less than the number of shrink operations necessary to remove any given pixel. The first shrink removes the boundary pixels i.e. points at distance 0 from the background; the next shrink removes points at distance 1, and so on. If you replace the value of each pixel by its distance from the background, the result is a sort of distance or depth map of the object (see Fig. 6.14).

The MAT is now very easy to derive from this depth map and consists of all the pixels with a depth which is a local maximum. That is, a pixel is part of the MAT if it has no neighbours with a distance value larger than its own value. Notice that if a 4-distance has been used, then neighbours should be taken to mean 4 neighbours and similarly if 8-distance has been used then a pixel's 8 neighbours should be considered.

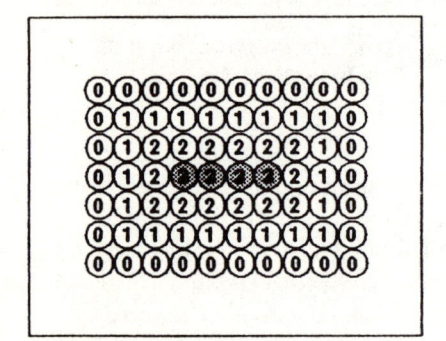

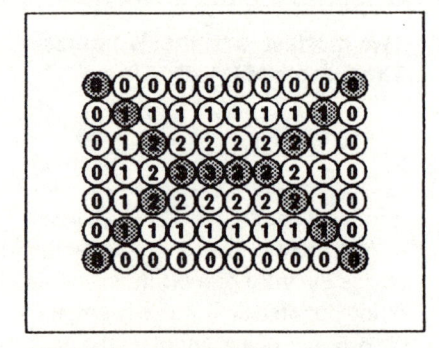

8 Connected MAT   **4 Connected MAT**

⬤ = pixel with no larger 8 – connected neighbour   ⬤ = pixel with no larger 4 – connected neighbour

Fig. 6.15 A MAT

Given the points in the MAT and their depths it is possible to reconstruct the object by expanding each point once more than its depth and ORing all the results together. Expanding each point surrounds it by a 'disk' of radius d and the object is the union of all these separate disks. It can be shown that the MAT is the smallest set of distance values from which the object can be reconstructed so any other type of skeleton from which the object can be reconstructed will have more, not fewer, points.

Shrinking and expanding also give a simple way of computing the MAT that is particularly suited to parallel computers. A point that is part of the MAT is characterised by the fact that it disappears following a shrink and does not reappear following an expand. To be more precise, a point in the

MAT at depth d disappears after d+1 shrinks and one expand. For a serial computer it is faster to construct the depth map and find local maxima.

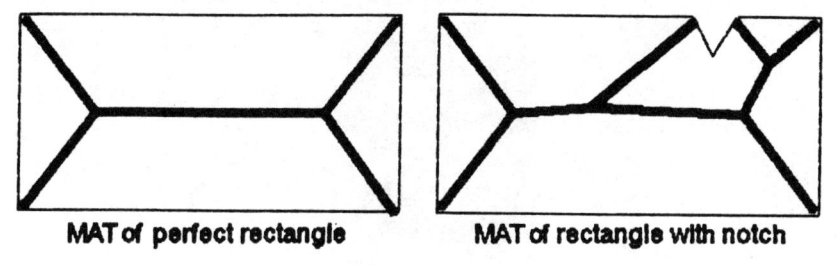

MAT of perfect rectangle **MAT of rectangle with notch**

Fig. 6.16 Problems with the MAT

The MAT is a simple skeleton but it has a number of problems (see Fig. 6.16). Roughly speaking, each lobe on the object corresponds to a branch on the MAT and this is a desirable property, but the MAT is very sensitive to small irregularities in the object and it may not form a connected set of pixels. There have been a number of attempts to obtain better behaved skeletons by not deleting border pixels during a shrink that would alter the connectedness of the object. The result is a skeleton which has the same connectedness as the object, i.e. the skeleton will be in one piece if the object is!

Subroutines to compute the depth map and the MAT

The following subroutine can be used to compute the depth map of any objects in the array bi%, storing the result in dbi% both nn% by nn%. Each time the subroutine is called, a standard shrink operation is performed on bi% and the result is stored in obi%. Any pixel that vanishes during this shrink operation is set to n% in the array dbi%. If n% is set at the number of times that the subroutine has been called to repeatedly shrink the image, the array dbi% is slowly set to the depth of every foreground pixel. The value of fin% can be used to test when the repeated shrink operations have removed all the foreground pixels; fin%=1 when every pixel in bi% is a background pixel and 0 otherwise.

```
SUB dshrink(bi%(2),obi%(2),
            dbi%(2),nn%,n%,fin%) STATIC
 REM set flag
 fin%=1
 FOR x%=1 TO nn%-2
  FOR y%=1 TO nn%-2
   REM do shrink
   b%=(NOT bi%(x%-1,y%)) OR (NOT bi%(x%+1,y%))
   b%=b% OR (NOT bi%(x%,y%-1))
       OR (NOT bi%(x%,y%+1))
```

126 *Pattern Recognition*

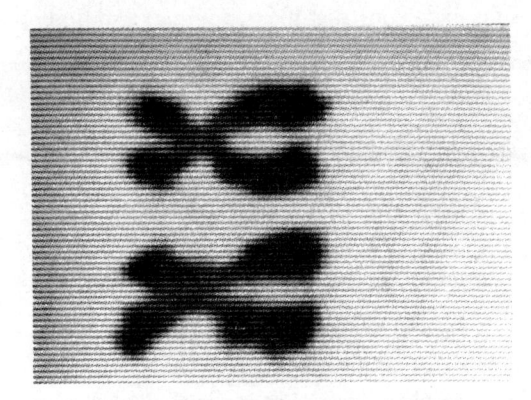

(a) Original image of chromosomes

(b) Binary image derived from original

Plate 11 Skeletonisation – 1

Binary Images 127

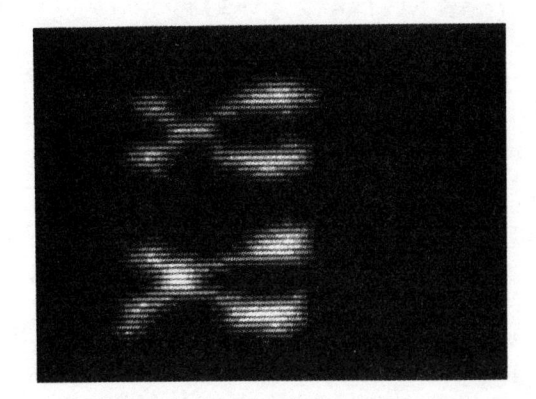

(c) Depth field

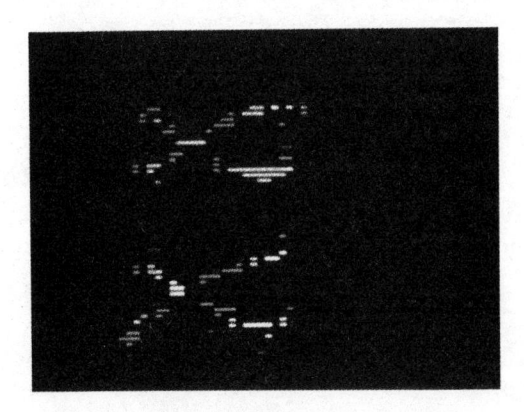

(d) Skeleton

128 Pattern Recognition

```
        b%=b% OR (NOT bi%(x%-1,y%-1))
            OR (NOT bi%(x%-1,y%+1))
        b%=b% OR (NOT bi%(x%+1,y%-1))
            OR (NOT bi%(x%+1,y%+1))
        obi%(x%,y%)=bi%(x%,y%) AND NOT b%
        REM set dbi% to n% if the
            pixel value has changed
        IF bi%(x%,y%)<>obi%(x%,y%) THEN
            fin%=0:dbi%(x%,y%)=n%
      NEXT y%
    NEXT x%
END SUB
```

The following subroutine will compute the MAT from the depth map produced by the previous subroutine by finding the local maxima. The depth map is stored in dbi% and the resulting MAT is returned in obi% both n% by n%.

```
SUB mat(dbi%(2),obi%(),nn%) STATIC
  FOR x%=1 TO nn%-2
    FOR y%=1 TO nn%-2
      obi%(x%,y%)=dbi%(x%,y%)
      FOR xi%=-1 TO 1
        FOR yi%=-1 TO 1
          IF dbi%(x%+xi%,y%+yi%)>dbi%(x%,y%) THEN
            obi%(x%,y%)=0
        NEXT yi%
      NEXT xi%
    NEXT y%
  NEXT x%
END SUB
```

An example of part of a main program to use these two subroutines to compute the MAT is given below

```
REM get image binary (true/false)
    image into bi%
REM set flag fin% and shrink counter n%
fin%=0:n%=1
REM repeatedly shrink image until it vanishes
WHILE fin%=0
  REM shrink bi% into obi%
  CALL shrink2(bi%(),obi%(),dbi%(),nn%,n%,fin%)
  n%=n%+1
```

```
REM shrink obi% into bi%
CALL shrink2(obi%(),bi%(),dbi%(),nn%,n%,fin%)
n%=n%+1
WEND
CALL mat(dbi%(),obi%(),nn%)
REM display the MAT in obi%
    and the depth map in dbi%
```

Counting and separating multiple objects

Most of the processing of binary images is concerned with smoothing the image or with separating it into different unconnected objects, so that measurements can be taken of single objects to enable them to be recognised, counted or sized. For example, if you were trying to count the number of blood cells in a sample, you might have managed to obtain a binary image showing each cell as a binary object, but how do you then count how many such objects there are?

The first part of this problem is that different objects in the image may overlap and to be counted they have to be separated. This is quite difficult for general objects but, if we know that all the objects are blobs that tend to overlap only slightly, they can be separated by repeated use of the shrink expand operators. Repeated use of the shrink operator removes any elongations or thin necks that might accidentally connect different objects. Expanding restores the objects to their original size and fills any holes. If you want to extract the original objects but without the thin projections and necks that might have connected them together then you can use the results of the expand operation as a mask by ANDing it with the original image.

Once you have separated the objects in an image you can count how many there are and even extract each one for further processing by *labelling* (see Fig. 6.18). This is achieved by scanning the image starting from the top left-hand corner and working across and down the image. The first time a foreground pixel, i.e. a 1, is encountered, it is assigned a label, 'A' say. After this each foreground pixel which is encountered is either assigned the same label as the pixel above or to its left or, if they are both background pixels, is assigned a new label. At the end of the scan all the objects are labelled but some objects may have more than one label! To correct this a second scan is necessary to identify any pixel label that has a neighbour with a different label and to change one of them. All that remains is to count the number of different symbols which is equal to the number of objects in the image.

An alternative method of labelling is based on the idea of *propagation*. Starting a scan from the top left-hand corner, as described above, the first

130 *Pattern Recognition*

(a) Original image of a leaf

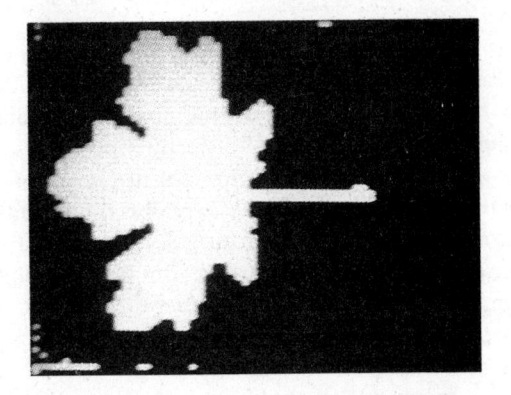

(b) Binary image derived from original

Plate 12 Skeletonisation – 2

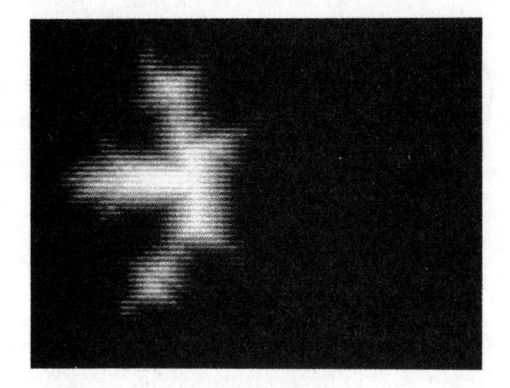

(c) Depth field

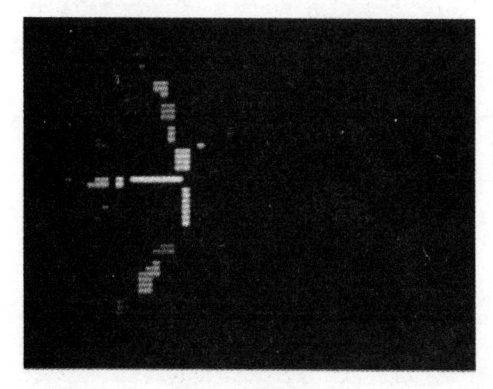

(d) Skeleton

132 *Pattern Recognition*

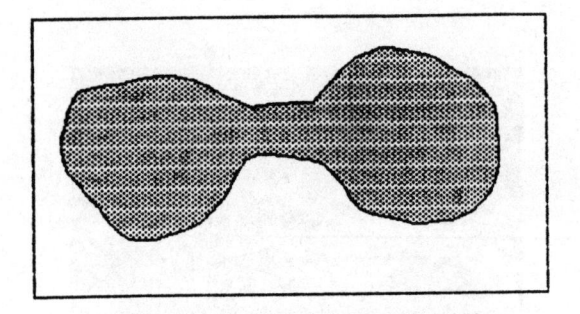

Two objects connected by a 'neck'

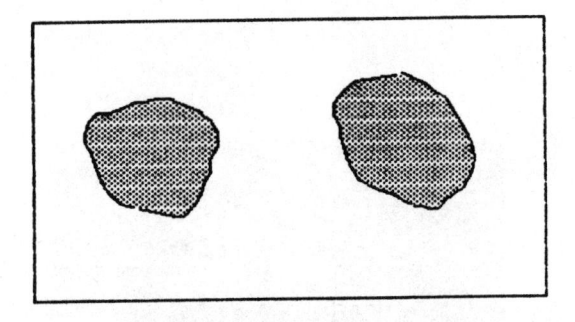

After sufficient shrink operations the neck disappears

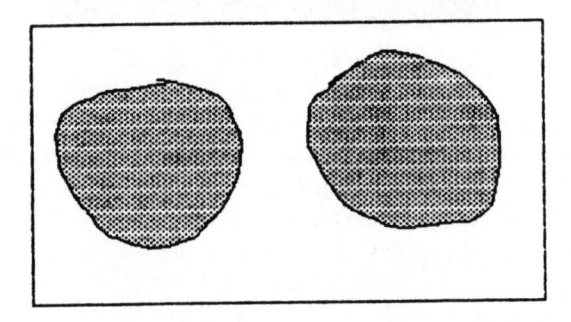

After expanding – two separate objects

Fig. 6.17 Separating objects using shrink expand

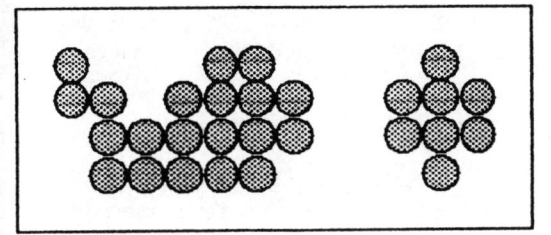

Two 4 connected objects

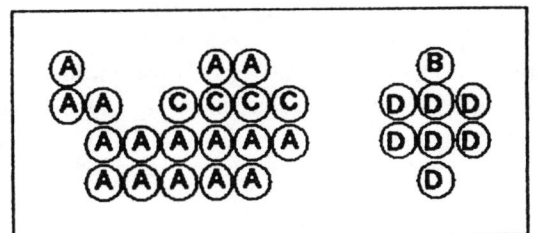

Labels assigned after a single scan

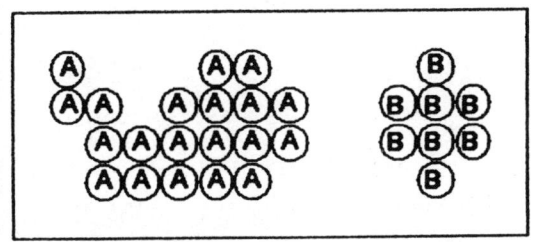

After the identification of C = A and D = B each object has a single unique label

Fig. 6.18 Labelling

foreground point encountered is assigned a label, 'A' say, the scan is temporarily halted and each foreground neighbour of the point in question is assigned the same label, then similarly with each of their neighbours and so on until there are no more unlabelled foreground neighbours. Then the scan is restarted until an unlabelled foreground pixel is found when a new label is issued, the scan halted and all its foreground neighbours are assigned the same label and so on until the entire image is scanned and all the objects are labelled. Although this propagation scheme sounds easy it is quite difficult to devise an efficient algorithm for checking all the foreground pixels connected to a given pixel by other foreground pixels.

A particularly simple method of counting the number of objects in an image is based on the *genus* or *Euler number G* but it only works for *simply connected* objects, i.e. those which do not have any holes. The genus is the number of objects minus the number of holes which they contain, and it can be calculated using:

$$G = T + HV - D$$

where T is the total number of foreground pixels, HV is the number of horizontal or vertical pairs of foreground pixels and D is the number of diagonal pairs of foreground pixels. (This formula assumes that the objects are 4-connected. A similar forumla exists for 8-connected objects.) Clearly, T, HV and D can be computed from a single scan of the image and therefore, as long as the objects can be guaranteed not to contain holes, G is a very fast way of computing the number of objects in the image. The biggest problem in image processing of this sort is finding fast methods of achieving results which seem obvious to a human viewing the image.

Postscript

There are many approaches to pattern recognition and image processing that have not even been mentioned, let alone described, in the six chapters of this book. One of the biggest problems is that with this multiplicity of approaches one can spend a great deal of time working on advanced theories and operators that produce almost identical results when applied to a digitised image. It is important to keep in mind at all times the object of the exercise. There is little point in designing a better and more complex feature detector if one of the standard simple operators performs well enough for the rest of the pattern recognition procedure to be successful.

The goal of pattern recognition

It is tempting to evaluate feature detectors in terms of how well they 'improve', in some vague sense, the appearance of a test image. For example, if you are developing a line detector then it is of interest to see how well it performs on an image containing some lines typical of those encountered in the real problem. Looking at the output of such an operator is often very misleading unless you are aware of the potential traps prepared by our own exceptionally good internal pattern recognition system. If you look at the original image, then your perception of the lines that it contains is the result of the most sophisticated image processing that we know of. Thus, you shouldn't be surprised if on examination of the results of your simple line detector it fails to find complete lines that to you are entirely obvious. On a closer examination you will probably find that the lines that are so obvious are in fact discontinuous and have regions of indistinctness that your visual processing has sucessfully filled in. On the other hand it is also likely that your line detector indicates apparently spurious short line segments that again upon closer inspection of the original prove to be real. In many ways designing and evaluating image processing operators is a constant battle with our own overly-efficient and powerful recognition system!

Keeping the ultimate goal of an image processing system in mind while working on the early stages of feature extraction can be particularly difficult if that goal is image recognition. For example, the problem of character recognition has been mentioned a number of times in early chapters but by the last chapter it is all too easy to think in terms of line detectors etc. While applying a line detector to a page of printed characters does improve the readability of a page of characters for a human it does little to advance the machine along the same road. In the same way, using an edge detector may make the outline of a car more visible but it doesn't make the job of detecting the presence of a car in the image very much easier.

There is a tendency to spend a great deal of time developing operators that improve the visiblity of some feature within the image, and then look at it and say 'now what?' Recognition implies the use of a classification rule; this in turn implies that the local feature detectors used supply it with a vector of numbers that serve to discriminate between the various groups. If a local operator improves the apparent visibility of a feature then it is a good bet that it provides a possible route to providing at least some of the information needed for a classification rule to operate sucessfully. For example, if you are trying to decide if a satellite image contains a road, then a first stage classifier might be constructed by applying a line detector and then counting the number of high values produced. If the object of the exercise is classification then the only measure of success is the performance of the classification rule not any apparent enhancement of the image.

Are we going in the right direction?

The approach used in this book can broadly be termed an engineering one in the sense that the task of pattern recognition has been taken to be a problem in computer science and artificial intelligence. This is not a universal view point and many workers subscribe to the view that pattern recognition should be considered to be a branch of psychology or biology because the only really successful pattern recognition systems that we know of are biological in their construction. Mostly such approaches lead to methods that are interesting but not practical.

The biology versus engineering argument is part of a wider split within all artificial intelligence. In practice there is no need to consider one approach to be correct at the expense of the other. The study of biological systems may one day show us how to construct better programs or machines, but at the moment the results only hint at very vague and either very general or ultra-specific principles. At the moment the best mixture of biology and engineering is to be found in computational vision as expouned by Marr (see

Further Reading). I can only say that everyone interested in computer vision should know something of this approach, if only for a glimpse of what a theory of vision might be like. The idea of a complete theory is something that we all cherish, but the absence of one should not be used as a reason for thinking that current methods lack power or are in any way unworkable. The methods that we currently have will not be invalidated by any subsequent discovery of an all-embracing theory; they are practical and provide the results we need.

Further Reading

This section has been included for the information of readers who wish to pursue any of the topics in this book. It is not intended to be comprehensive and does not include reference to individual papers. Rather it provides starting points for further study in each of the major areas listed.

Image processing
Baxes, G.A. (1984) *Digital Image Processing: A Practical Primer*. Prentice-Hall.
Niblack, W. (1986) *An Introduction to Digital Image Processing*. Prentice-Hall International.
Pratt, W.K (1978) *Digital Image Processing*. Prentice-Hall.

Image processing as applied to pattern recognition
Nevatia, R. (1982) *Machine Perception*. Prentice-Hall.
Rosenfeld, A. (1969) *Picture Processing by Computer*. Academic Press.
Rosenfeld, A. and Kak, A.C. (1982) *Digital Picture Processing*. 2nd edn. Vols 1 and 2. Academic Press.
Rosenfeld, A. and Lipkin, B.S. (1970) *Picture Processing and Psychopictorics*. Academic Press.

Classification and pattern recognition
James, M. (1985) *Classification Algorithms*. Collins.
Andrews, H.C. (1972) *Introduction to Mathematical Techniques in Pattern Recognition*. Wiley-Interscience.
Fukanaga, K. (1972) *Introduction to Statistical Pattern Recognition*. Academic Press.

Computational vision
Marr, D. (1982) *Vision*. W. H. Freeman & Co.

Digital signal processing
Gold, B. and Rader, C.M. (1969) *Digital Processing of Signals*. McGraw-Hill.

Statistics

Chatfield, C. and Collins, A.J. (1980) *Introduction to Multivariate Statistics*. Chapman and Hall.

Searle, S.R. (1971) *Linear Models*. John Wiley & Sons.

Artificial intelligence

Jackson, P.C. (1985) *Introduction to Artificial Intelligence*. 2nd edn. Dover.

James, M. (1986) *BASIC Artificial Intelligence*. Butterworths.

Computer graphics

Newman, W.M. and Sproull, R.F. (1979) *Principles of Interactive Computer Graphics*. McGraw-Hill.

Collections of papers

Agarwala, A.K. (1976) *'Machine Recognition of Patterns'*. IEEE Computer Society Press.

Chellappa, R. and Sawchuk, A.A. (1985) *'Digital Image Processing and Analysis'*. Vols 1 and 2. IEEE Computer Society Press.

The British Pattern Recognition Society

The British Pattern Recognition Society, BPRA, is the main forum for ideas in pattern recognition and image processing as it applies to pattern recognition. Further details can be obtained from:

The Membership Secretary
British Pattern Recognition Association
Department of Physics and Astronomy
University College London
Gower Street
London WC1E 6BT.

Suggested Projects

Image acquisition and display

(1) If you have an image input and display device, write subroutines to store a digitised image in an array and then display it.

(2) Write a subroutine that will generate a test image, stored in an array, of an edge with the facility to add noise.

(3) Write a subroutine to display a grey level image using your computer's graphics capabilities. (Either plot dots in various colours or vary the number of dots that you print to achieve a range of grey tones.)

Classification

(4) Produce a demonstration program for the linear training algorithm in two dimensions. Generate random data for the two groups, draw a scatter diagram and the dividing line. Show how the line moves at each iteration by plotting it on the diagram.

(5) Add to the program produced in project (4) a plot of the linear discriminant function so that it can be compared with the dividing line produced by the linear training algorithm.

Local feature detection

(6) Use mask matching to detect and mark the letter A in an image containing a number of possible letters.

(7) Design and implement a local feature detector for a round blob-like feature.

(8) Design and implement a set of local feature detectors for lines of a range of widths.

(9) Investigate the ways in which the outputs from the local feature detectors in (8) could be combined.

142 Pattern Recognition

Frequency methods

(10) Improve the efficiency of the FFT subroutine given in Chapter Four by making it work directly on the two-dimensional array.

(11) Use the FFT to implement a convolution of a mask with an image.

(12) Take the Fourier transform of a simple edge, subject it to a high pass filter and then take the inverse transform. Try to design a filter that makes the edge sharper.

Segmentation

(13) Implement the relaxation threshold method described in Chapter Five.

(14) Evaluate the three texture measures, given in Chapter Five, on a number of different texture samples. Try to construct a linear classifier based on the co-occurrence matrices.

(15) Try to classify textures using features extracted from their spectrum.

Binary images

(16) Design a local operator to remove dark isolated pixels.

(17) Write a program that extracts the boundary pixels in an image using a border-following algorithm – that is, by finding a pixel in the border and then tracking it around the object. Is this more efficient than the equivalent Boolean local operator?

(18) Implement object counting by using the genus number.

(19) Write a program that will classify a number of simple shapes using generalised pi. Extend the program so that it uses moments as well.

(20) Write a subroutine that will turn a boundary into a chain code and vice versa.

Index

aliasing, 74
area, 116

Bayes' law, 22
Bayes' rule, 21, 32
binary filtering, 113, 114
   images, 10, 102
   mask matching, 117
   object, 103
bivariate normal, 24
Boolean operator, 102, 106, 109
boundary, 107

chain code, 122
classification, 15, 19
colour, 3
conditional probability, 21
connectivity, 107
convolution, 38, 40, 76, 87, 117
co-occurence matrix, 96
correlation coefficient, 36, 42
counting, 129

decision line, 25
decision tree, 32
depth map, 124
digitisation, 5
discrete Fourier transform, 66

edge detection, 41, 46
eight-connected, 107
elliptical symmetry, 27
Euler number, 133

expand, 113

feature extraction, 20
fast Fourier transform, 67
   and sampling, 73
filtering, 76, 80, 87
four-connected, 107
Fourier transform, 63
frequency aliasing, 73
frequency methods, 63
functions, 4

genus, 133
gradient methods, 44
grey level image, 4
grey level quantisation, 7

Hadamard transform, 81
hardware, 15
histogram, 10, 11
Hough transform, 88
Hueckel operator, 49
hum bars, 82

image enhancement, 3, 77
   processing, 1, 2, 6
   restoration, 3, 77
   understanding, 19
isolated points, 112

Karhunen-Loeve transform, 81

144 Index

labelling, 129
Laplacian operator, 57
least squares, 46
linear classification, 26, 27
linear discriminant, 26, 28, 30
linear model, 46
line detection, 53, 88
local boolean operators, 109
local feature, 35
   detection, 35, 60
   statistics, 100

mask matching, 117
MAT, 123
medial axis, 122
   transformation, 123
model fitting, 46
moments, 116
multiple correlation, 47

non-linear detectors, 60
non-maximum suppression, 61
normal distribution, 22, 23
Nyquist rate, 6, 74

optical transform, 75
optimal filtering, 80

p4, 110, 117
p8, 110, 117
paint process, 9
perception, 30
perimeter, 110, 116
phase, 64
photometric correction, 10
pixel, 6
power spectrum, 65
predicate functions, 14
Prewitt's operator, 45
prior probability, 22

probability, 21

quadratic classification, 26
quantisation, 7

region growing, 84
region splitting, 84
relaxation, 90
Robert's gradient, 44, 45

sample space, 25
sampling effects, 73
scale, 61
second derivature, 55
segmentation, 84
separating opjects, 129
Shannon's sampling theory, 6
shape, 116, 121
shrink, 113
singular value decomposition, 81
skeletonisation, 112
smoothing, 87
Sobel's operator, 45
spatial frequency, 63
spatial quantisation, 6
spectral density, 81
spectrum, 64
statistics, 21

template matching, 36, 38
texture, 92
threshold selection, 11, 85
threshold value, 11
training, 30
two-dimensional fast Fourier
   transform, 72

Wiener filtering, 80